I0087806

SHAKESPEARE RE-PLAYED:
Two Shakespearean Travesties

SHAKESPEARE RE-PLAYED:
Two Shakespearean Travesties

Falstaff in Rebellion

Re-Taming of the Shrew

WILDSIDE PRESS

SHAKESPEARE RE-PLAYED

Published by:

Wildside Press
P.O. Box 301
Holicong, PA 18928-0301 USA
www.wildsidepress.com

This edition copyright © 2003 by Wildside Press.
All rights reserved.

CONTENTS

Falstaff in Rebellion

or

The Mutineers of Eastcheap

A Shakespearian Travesty in Three Acts

by

JOHN W. POSTGATE

CHARACTERS

Sir John Falstaff.
William Shakespeare.
Ben Jonson.
Sir Toby Belch.
Robert Greene.
Nym.
Bardolph.
Pistol.
Captain Bobadil.
Mercutio.
Shylock.
King Claudius.
Hamlet's Ghost.
Macbeth.
Bottom.
Polonius.
Dogberry.
Verges.
Mark Antony.
Othello.
Francis.
Ostlers.
Malvolio.
Mrs. Quickly.
Lady Macbeth.
Maria.
Viola.
Desdemona.
Ophelia.

SYNOPSIS

Falstaff in Rebellion

ACT I

SCENE.—*The Boar's Head Tavern.*

*[*NYM, BARDOLPH *and* PISTOL *discovered drinking at table,* FRANCIS *serving them. They pledge each other in silence, and sigh heavily as they set down the cups.]*

[Enter MRS. QUICKLY.*]*

MRS. QUICKLY: Thus it goes from morn to night; nothing but groans and sighs and sack. And what a merry place it was before Sir John parted. They must be roused or they'll drink the cellar dry. Come, brave hearts, give sorrow words! The grief that does not speak is bound to knock you all a-heap.

PISTOL: Ah!

NYM: Oh!

BARDOLPH: Ah! those happy, happy days!

PISTOL: So true, so kind, so valiant!

NYM: Slow to anger, yet quick to reward!

BARDOLPH: His heart too big for his body.

PISTOL: His hand in every purse.

NYM: Ah! that's the humor of it.

MRS. QUICKLY: He's in Arthur's bosom, if ever man went there.

BARDOLPH: Would I were with him wheresoever he is, whether in heaven or hell.

PISTOL: Bring more solace, Francis.

*[*FRANCIS *replenishes the cups. They drink in silence, sighing as they place them empty on the table. Door up stage opens and* SIR JOHN FALSTAFF *appears on the threshold and looks on the scene.]*

[15]

But soft, lambkins! Methinks I scent the outer air.

[All turn toward the door and spring up in fright.]

NYM: Angels and ministers of grace defend us!

BARDOLPH: Be thou a spirit of health or goblin damned?

PISTOL: Bringst with thee airs from heaven or blasts from hell?

FALSTAFF: *[advancing].* Brave hearts, I am with ye once again!

[They all rush out in fear.]

This is a wondrous strange welcome. Am I the plague that they avoid me so? But such is the state of man. One day the glad hand, the next the marble heart. My throat is as arid as a deviled bone. Francis!

MRS. QUICKLY: *[within].* Go to it, good Francis; be not afeard.

FALSTAFF: Francis, I say!

FRANCIS: *[within].* Anon, anon, sir.

FALSTAFF: Confound thy parrot tongue! Bring me a cup of sack. Stand not upon the order of coming, but come at once.

MRS. QUICKLY: *[within].* Sack! It must have sack! Go, good Francis, go!

*[Enter **FRANCIS** with wine; places cup on table, and retreats hurriedly. **FALSTAFF** takes a deep draught.]*

FALSTAFF: Ah, you rogue, there's lime in this sack! Is there no virtue extant in villainous man? Shall I not get honest wine at mine inn? Bring me a cup of sack, you rogue; pure vintage, you had best!

MRS. QUICKLY: *[within].* Oh, run, good Francis, run! Fill full from the other barrel. Would that the cock would crow!

*[Reënter **FRANCIS** with wine; retreats as before.]*

FALSTAFF: *[after drinking]*. Ah! that trickles to the spot! I must consider of my circumstances; there seems to be a changed atmosphere here. After all my pains in his training, to think that Hal should immure me in the Fleet with villains vile and rank. And all for nothing! For a simple ebullition of my heartfelt love and eternal devotion. Why did I leave Master Shallow's orchard? Why did I rush to the coronation? I should have known that it is unwise to put trust in princes. There's nothing now but to settle down with Dame Quickly among foaming bottles and ale-washed wits.

> *[Enter* ROBERT GREENE.*]*

GREENE: God ye good den, Sir John.

FALSTAFF: Ah, Master Greene; is it good den?

GREENE: It is, your worship; the sun is in its meridian.

FALSTAFF: Then is the sun in better case than I. Gadzooks, Master Greene, we young men are no conservators of time. We burn the Standard Oil at both ends; we procrastinate, we wax indifferent; 'tis the inalienable prerogative, the roseate province of youth. But our thirst is always with us, Master Greene; that is a perennial blessing, for which we should be devoutly thankful. Princes and lords may flourish or may fade, but a thirst once acquired is never allayed. Francis!

FRANCIS: *[within]*. Anon, anon, sir.

FALSTAFF: Bring two cups of wine, you muddy rascal.

> *[Reënter* FRANCIS *with cups, and exit as before.* FALSTAFF *offers a cup to* GREENE, *who shudders.]*

GREENE: You must excuse me, Sir John; I have drank and seen the spider!

FALSTAFF: What, man! Never tell me thou hast foresworn sack and sugar.

GREENE: 'Tis true, your honor.

FALSTAFF: Then 'tis pity, Master Greene. *[Drinks.]* Lord, how the world changes! I suppose we'll have universal prohibition next. They've already started it in the old Southern States, where erstwhile the mint julep was the merry cheerer of every true gentleman's heart. What next, I wonder? Mayhap when I grow old myself, I'll purge and leave sack and live cleanly as a nobleman should do. But while youth and vigor last, Master Greene, and there's no obstruction in my gullet, I'll drink carouses to the next day's fate. *[Drinks again.]* Ah! balm of Gilead! But what make you here, Master Greene? This is no place for a teetotaler.

GREENE: I came to learn from your own lips, Sir John, whether William Shakespeare, when you wooed our hostess here, knew of your love.

FALSTAFF: He did; he planned the soulful scenes, and framed the dulcet dialogue with which we wooed.

GREENE: Indeed.

FALSTAFF: Indeed, ay, indeed! Discern'st thou aught in that contrary to the canons of Christian courtship? Is he not honest?

GREENE: Sir John, for aught I know.

FALSTAFF: What dost thou think?

GREENE: Think, Sir John?

FALSTAFF: Think, Sir John. By heaven, he echoes me, as if there was some monster in his thought too hideous to be shown. Now, Master Greene, I like not this style of dialogue; it savors too much of that blackamoor tomfoolery at the Globe theatre. How far thou resemblest honest Iago is not for me to say; but I think 'tis plainly apparent that I am not built on Othello's plan. My occupation may be in jeopardy for the nonce, but it hasn't gone yet; and, moreover, I do not propose to annihilate myself for any guinea hen in all Christendom. Now, what is't thou art driving at?

GREENE: Oh, beware, Sir John, of jealousy; it is the green-eyed monster—

FALSTAFF: Fudge, Master Greene! I am not to be moved by the fustian. Hast not heard of Doll Tearsheet? Thinkest thou I'd make a life of jealousy to follow still the changes of the moon with fresh suspicion on her account? Art not acquainted with Mistress Page and Mistress Ford, the merry wives of Windsor? My affections never anchor long enough for jealousy to sprout, Master Greene; they skip lightly from flower to flower in the garden of beauty. I love them all, Master Greene, I love them all! Would that womankind had but one mouth, I'd kiss them all from North to South.

GREENE: 'Tis of Mistress Quickly I would speak, your honor.

FALSTAFF: And what of Mistress Quickly?

GREENE: While you languished in prison, Sir John, Shakespeare inveigled her to report that a burning quotidian fever was gnawing at thy vitals. Then, in due course, she circulated a rumor that thou hadst died of a broken heart, with a nose as sharp as a pen, and babbling o' greenfields. Oh, Sir John, it was pitiful, 'twas pitiful.

FALSTAFF: An he did that, by Saint Patrick, it was damnable. But I know you, Master Greene; I have heard of they Groats-worth of Wit. Thou art no friend of Shakespeare.

GREENE: Curse him, no! But your own followers can resolve you as to the truth of what I have imparted.

FALSTAFF: By heaven, a light begins to dawn. You say that Master Shakespeare killed me?

GREENE: He did, indeed, Sir John. You are as dead as a door-nail in his estimation.

FALSTAFF: Then, being dead, what should I be?

GREENE: The shade of your former self; a flimsy, shadowy, fleshless ghost.

FALSTAFF: A ghost! Ha, ha! A beggarly, revenge-shrieking shade. Well, I flatter myself there is not much ghost about this goodly corporation. Ha, ha! A ghost forsooth! Did ever ghost drink as much sack as I to-day? Then that's why the lads slunk away from me. Ha, ha! Call them in, Master Greene; call them in; 'tis time we disabused their imaginations.

GREENE: *[going to door]*. Nym, Bardolph, Pistol!

[They peer timidly out.]

Come forth, bully rooks! 'Tis Sir John himself in his habit as he lived.

[Enter NYM, BARDOLPH, *and* PISTOL; *they salute* FALSTAFF.*]*

NYM, BARDOLPH, and PISTOL: Hail, noble imp of fame!

FALSTAFF: Brave hearts and bold! We will celebrate this glorious resurrection. Again shall we hear the chimes at midnight. We shall despoil rich chuffs of predatory wealth; we shall smash the monopolistic trusts. And nobles shall ye have, and present pay, and good red liquor besides, oceans of it. Cups shall not be scanted. We will bathe in Malmsey and swim in sack!

NYM, BARDOLPH, and PISTOL: Hurrah!

FALSTAFF: But tell me, lads; did ye really think I was dead?

PISTOL: She told us gently thou wert dead, and we did yearn therefore.

FALSTAFF: She? Who?

BARDOLPH: Dame Quickly, your honor.

FALSTAFF: Quickly! Oh, sit still, my heart, and you, my sinews, grow not instant old, but bear me stiffly on my pins. Quickly! Alas! 'Twas thus he lured the Scottish chieftain to his doom. The words come home to me now. If 'twere done when 'twere done, then 'twere well 'twere done, Quickly! O frailty! thy name is Quickly!

[Enter MRS. QUICKLY.*]*

MRS. QUICKLY: Oh, dear Sir John, how grateful I am to see thee back from the grave, with clothes on and in thy right mind, with the breath of life in thy nostrils, too, just as it was in the Dolphin chamber by the sea coal fire at—

FALSTAFF: Peace, wicked woman! 'Twas thou that made my winding sheet.

MRS. QUICKLY: Indeed, indeed, Sir John, I was as innocent as the lifeless babe unborn. 'Twas that rogue, Will Shakespeare. He it was that told me to heap clothes on the bed, and to feel thy feet and thy knees and thy pulsidge, and all was really as cold as any stone, Sir John.

FALSTAFF: Well, clear thy crystals, Nell; no doubt thy tender heart was imposed upon. When I have settled with Master Shakespeare, I will speak with thee on those happy themes of yore.

GREENE: Moreover, after your alleged death, Sir John—

FALSTAFF: What! was there something after death? Was not the villain satisfied with my murder in cold blood?

GREENE: On the glorious field of Agincourt, where your valor would have added luster to the victory, he put words of bitter derogation into the mouth of Fluellen.

PISTOL: An ill-smelling, leek-eating Welshman, Sir John.

FALSTAFF: Ah! And what did he make that Welsh rabbit say?

GREENE: That Harry Monmouth, when he came to his right wits and judgment, did right in turning down the knight with the great belly doublet—the fat man that was full of jests and gipes and knaveries and mocks—he had forgot his name.

FALSTAFF: Forgot my name! Forgot Falstaff! I'll carve it on his beggarly hide! I'll have it put into double and treble consonants, and bawled into his ear while he is asleep! Forgot my name! Kind heaven! help me to contain myself!

GREENE: Patience, Sir John, patience!

FALSTAFF: I'll chop him into ten thousand pieces.

GREENE: Ay, but that might kill him, and Kit Marlowe says death ends all. We must not be so lenient with him. We must devise something lingering and torturing; we must make him suffer in proportion to his crimes. Suppose we plague him with his own inventions?

FALSTAFF: Plague him?

GREENE: Ay, stir his own chickens to revolt—irritate them against him. You, Sir John, have not been the only victim of Shakespeare's venomous spleen; he has maligned and stabbed other worthy gentlemen. There's Macbeth, for instance, and Mercutio, Sir Toby Belch, my lord Hamlet, Shylock the Jew, the noble Antony, and a score of others he has belittled and defamed. Several of them I have already sounded and they are ripe for revolt. They will join hands with you, Sir John, and you can make the last days of Will Shakespeare more wretched than his first.

FALSTAFF: The plot pleases me. We will proclaim him in the streets; poison his pleasures, incense his wife, madden his kinsmen, and set his mother-in-law upon him. We will throw such changes of vexation into his life that he will wish he had ne'er been born.

PISTOL: His vertical column shall be ripped from its base.

NYM: That's the humor of it!

GREENE: No time should be lost. Give him no warning. Take him grossly, full of bread, with all his crimes broad blown, as flush as May. Trip him so that his heels may kick at heaven, and his soul may be damned and black as hell!

NYM, BARDOLPH, and PISTOL: We shall, bully rook, we shall!

FALSTAFF: Then about it at once, brave hearts; some one way, some another. Call everybody who has a grievance and a spirit for revenge. I will spend but a moment with our hostess here, and will be with you straight.

[Exit FALSTAFF *with* MRS. QUICKLY. NYM, BARDOLPH, *and* PISTOL *draw their swords and strut out in single file by the up-stage door.]*

GREENE: Now let it work; mischief, thou art afoot, take thou what course thou wilt. *[Exit.]*

[Enter MALVOLIO, *carrying a cloak and black mask.]*

MALVOLIO: This should be the place; a fit scene for black conspiracy and midnight horrors. I will absorb their plans and purposes and baffle their plots, and then will I smile and smile my way into the benign favor of Master Shakespeare. Ah! they come! I must be wary. *[Retires behind the arras.]*

[Reënter FALSTAFF *and* MRS. QUICKLY.]*

FALSTAFF: Ay, but to let me die, and go I know not where; to lie in dull cold obstruction and to rot; this sensible and portly frame to become a kneaded clod; to bathe in fiery floods, or to reside in thrilling regions of thick-ribbed ice; to be imprisoned in the viewless winds, and blown with restless violence about the pendent world.

MRS. QUICKLY: Oh, dear Sir John, I never thought it was so bad as all that; it makes my blood run frigidly to hear thee. But don't take on so, there's a good man; anything in reason will I do to make amends. Ah! how often did I dream about being my lady, thy wife, in those happy bygone days.

FALSTAFF: Well, say no more, sweet wench. Thou knowest I am a compassionate man, and I forgive thee freely. And as for that sweet dream of thine, belike it shall yet come true.

MRS. QUICKLY: Oh, never, Sir John, never; 'twas but a dream.

FALSTAFF: Ay, but it denoted a happy consummation though it was but a dream. Come, buss me, dame, buss me; and, I prithee, lend me thirty shillings.

MALVOLIO: *[peeping from arras].* Thus would he make his fool his purse!

MRS. QUICKLY: Nay, but it cannot be, Sir John, it cannot be; i' faith I cannot.

FALSTAFF: Cannot, sweet Quickly; in the lexicon of Cupid, there's no such word as cannot.

[MRS. QUICKLY buries her face in apron.]

MALVOLIO: She melts before the flame of that fat Cupid.

FALSTAFF: Why, look up, sweet hostess! Here am I, hale and hearty, though a little thin at the poll; full of life and vigor; a good portly man, of a cheerful look, a pleasing eye, and a most noble carriage; the same sweet and kind and true Jack Falstaff that wooed and won thee of yore.

MALVOLIO: The poor bird is limed!

FALSTAFF: Come buss me, dame, buss me with a constant heart. *[Offers to kiss her.]* Let it be forty shillings if thou canst.

[Enter PISTOL up-stage; starts on seeing the situation.]

PISTOL: Oh, hound of Crete! thinkst thou my spouse to get?

MRS. QUICKLY: Mercy! Pistol! My husband!

FALSTAFF: Zounds! her husband! Here's a kettle of fish!

PISTOL: *[with hand on sword].* From the powdered tub of infamy fetch forth the lazar kite of Cressid's kind, Doll Tearsheet she by name, and her espouse. I have and I will hold the quondam Quickly for the only she.

FALSTAFF: Why, my trusty ancient, this is grand, this is glorious news. But why conceal the espousal from old Jack? Why not invite me to the wedding? But still I am glad and proud and fortunate withal. I have now a double-barreled defense against drought and disaster—two pistols with but a single stock, two flagons that flow as one. Bless ye, my children; long life and happiness, and troops of good-paying guests.

PISTOL: 'Tis nobly said! I kiss they neif, sweet knight. Give him thy lips, my love!

[FALSTAFF kisses MRS. QUICKLY.*]*

MALVOLIO: Pshaw! A flash in the pan!

PISTOL: Caveto be thy counsellor. Remember the word is "pitch and pay": trust none.

[Exit MRS. QUICKLY.*]*

FALSTAFF: How found you our friends, Pistol?

PISTOL: Excellent well, i' faith; they roar like raging lions.

MALVOLIO: *[advancing with cloak and mask on disguised as* OTHELLO*].* Most potent, grave and reverend seigniors—

FALSTAFF: That sounds familiar. Ah! our old college chum, the dusky Othello. Welcome to Eastcheap, my lord.

MALVOLIO: That I have ta'en away this old man's daughter—

FALSTAFF: Forget that, Othello; cut it out!

MALVOLIO: The very head and front of my offending—

FALSTAFF: Yes, yes, we know all that. A magnificent speech, well phrased, aptly turned, and grandly majestic in its turgid flow of Ethiopian eloquence. But you have the wrong cue, Otto, my boy. The Senate has adjourned; Brabantio is dead; and this is the Boar's Head tavern, where wine and wassail combine with wit and wisdom to divert humdrum existence into rippling rivers of mirth and hilarity.

MALVOLIO: Oh, Desdemona! Oh! False to me, to me!

FALSTAFF: *[to* PISTOL*].* Get him poppy, or mandragora, or juice of cursed hebona in a vial—any old soporific to stop this raving. He'll spoil the play.

PISTOL: I'll fix his royal sootiness. *[Exit.]*

[Enter SIR TOBY BELCH, *singing.]*

SIR TOBY: Hail, Sir John; I trust I see thee well.

FALSTAFF: In fair sort, good Sir Toby; I breathe, I breathe still.

SIR TOBY: Oh, knight, thou lackest a cup of canary!

FALSTAFF: Anon, Sir Toby, anon. The management of this inn has changed, and I am a trifle uncertain as to my credit yet.

MALVOLIO: Look, if my gentle love be not raised up!

SIR TOBY: Why, bless my heart, what have we here?

FALSTAFF: 'Tis the black general, Othello. He was summoned to our conference, but I am afraid the bugs are still in his bonnet.

MALVOLIO: Cassio, I love thee, but never more be officer of mine!

[SIR TOBY, who has been watching **MALVOLIO** *intently, snatches off his mask.]*

SIR TOBY: A counterfeit knave! A thin-faced knave, a gull! Taste your legs, you rogue; put them in motion. *[Drives* **MALVOLIO** *out.]*

FALSTAFF: What! the mincing Malvolio!

MALVOLIO: *[returning].* I'll be revenged on the whole pack of you!

[SIR TOBY half draws his sword and **MALVOLIO** *runs out.]*

[Reënter **PISTOL** *with pillows.]*

PISTOL: Where is the colored warrior?

FALSTAFF: Vanished, Pistol. 'Twas the cross-gartered knave, Malvolio, in disguise. Sir Toby drove him hence.

PISTOL: That robs the Coroner of a fee! I was about to give the uncircumcised dog his own medicine. *[Throws away the pillows.]*

SIR TOBY: 'Tis better as it is. But this should be a lesson to us, Sir John. The colored man is a disturbing element in current politics and shoiuld be excluded from our councils.

FALSTAFF: It shall be as you say, Sir Toby; we have troubles enough of our own without assuming the black man's bundle. I'll pledge thee in a cup of sack, Sir Toby. Francis!

FRANCIS: *[within]*. Anon, anon, sir!

FALSTAFF: Bring wine, you rogue!

PISTOL: What money is in thy purse, Sir John?

FALSTAFF: Not a groat, Pistol, not a groat. I can find no remedy against this consumption of the purse; borrowing only lingers and lingers it out, but the disease is incurable.

PISTOL: Then a remedy must you find for consumption of sack; there's eight shillings to pay already.

FALSTAFF: Base is the slave that pays! Thy own saw, Pistol, thy own saw!

PISTOL: Ay, but the boot is on the other leg now. I'm landlord, and 'tis pay or thirst.

[Enter FRANCIS with wine; PISTOL motions him back.]

No mun, no sack!

FALSTAFF: Sirrah! bring hither the cups!

PISTOL: *[drawing sword]*. The grave doth gape and doting death is near.

FALSTAFF: *[drawing]*. Have I nursed a viper to my bosom? Egregious dog! I'll slice thy miserly throat.

PISTOL: Miser! The miser in thy most merveillous face; the miser in thy teeth and throat, and in thy hateful lungs, yea, in thy maw, perdy, and, which is worse, within thy nasty mouth! I thee defy!

SIR TOBY: *[going between]*. Put up your bright swords, or the dew will rust them! An thou sheathe not thy weapon, ancient Pistol, I'll run thee up to the hilts, as I am a soldier.

PISTOL: *[sheathing]*. An oath of mickle might; and fury shall abate; but wine flows not without the price.

SIR TOBY: Friendship must combine and brotherhood. Francis, deliver the cups.

[FRANCIS serves FALSTAFF and SIR TOBY.]

We must drink down all unkindness.

[They drink.]

Score this on me, Pistol.

[PISTOL goes to the door and chalks up figures. While he is doing so, enter MACBETH, SHYLOCK, LADY MACBETH, DOGBERRY, VERGES, MARK ANTONY, MERCUTIO, POLONIUS, BOTTOM, KING CLAUDIUS, HAMLET'S GHOST, NYM, BARDOLPH and MARIA. MRS. QUICKLY comes from side entrance.]

FALSTAFF: Welcome all, good friends; a hundred thousand welcomes.

[Attendants bring chairs and range them in semi-circle, like the set of a minstrel show. SIR TOBY and PISTOL take the ends; FALSTAFF takes the interlocutor's seat in center.]

Nym and Bardolph will see that the doors are secured, and tile the center portal.

[NYM and BARDOLPH obey instructions.]

PISTOL: How do you sagatiate this evening, Brother Toby?

SIR TOBY: Somewhat salubrious and suspicious, thank you, Brother Pistol. And what may be the mental and physical state of your corporosity?

PISTOL: Oh, I'se scrumptious and bumptious. Brother Toby, can you tell me when Shakespeare is not Shakespeare?

SIR TOBY: That's easy, Brother Pistol. Shakespeare is not Shakespeare when he lacks Bacon.

PISTOL: Why, Brother Toby, I'se surprised at your ignoramousness. There may be some hams here, but this is not a baconical convention. Try again, Brother Toby.

SIR TOBY: Well, Brother Pistol, if Shakespeare is himself without Bacon, I give it up. When is Shakespeare not Shakespeare, Brother Pistol?

PISTOL: When he is put on the stage.

[Characters laugh.]

I've another—

FALSTAFF: Come to order, gentlemen. This is an indignation meeting, not a minstrel show!

[Noise at C. door up stage, which opens and shows **OTHELLO** *trying to enter.* **NYM** *and* **BARDOLPH** *push him out and close the door.]*

Comrades in misfortune and companions in revenge: We have deemed it prudent at this crisis of the nation's history to disfranchise the colored voter. Henceforth, this is to be a white man's country.

ALL: Hurrah!

FALSTAFF: I am glad to hear this expression of unanimity and approval, for these be parlous times, and united we stand, divided we fall. In union there is strength.

CLAUDIUS: Not always, Mr. Chairman; the union I put in Hamlet's cup did not strengthen me.

HAMLET'S GHOST: Thank God for that. He doped me while sleeping in my orchard, my custom in the afternoon.

PISTOL: Oh, that's an old story. It needs no ghost to come from the grave to tell us that.

LADY MACBETH: Shame, shame!

MARIA: It's an outrage to vex a poor ghost.

HAMLET'S GHOST: Oh, don't mind me; I have no bones for words to bruise.

FALSTAFF: Ladies! Gentlemen! Restrain yourselves, I beg of you. Let private animosity and individual spite be replaced with magnanimity and devotion to the common weal. We have met on this occasion to make common cause against a general enemy—one who, to gratify rabid spleen and personal malice, has employed every implement of indignity and malignity known to practical politics; a man who, base born and low bred himself, is no respecter of persons; a man who twists and distorts historic truths for self-aggrandizement; a man who—

PISTOL: Name, name! Who is this Man Who?

FALSTAFF: 'Tis that deer-stealing, sheep-biting knave, Will Shakespeare.

ALL: Ah! ah!

FALSTAFF: Each and every one in convention here assembled, I opine, has been wrongfully abused by him.

MERCUTIO: I can answer for one. He cut me short in a career that promised mirth and laughter to the end of time. The wound was not as deep as a well, or as wide as a church door, but it served, it served!

MACBETH: And I can answer for another. He kept the word of promise to my ear but broke it to my hope. He stole mid-night hags and evil spells from Thomas Middleton to bewitch and betray and destroy me.

MARIA: He broke dear Sir Toby's head before we were married, and it has never been right since.

SIR TOBY: Nor never will be again, I'm afraid, while I am married.

MARIA: You wretch! wait till I get you home!

HAMLET'S GHOST: He sent me to purgatory, to fast in fires and do such stunts as the bitter day would quake to look upon.

CLAUDIUS: Would he had kept thee there forever, thou miserable night prowler.

HAMLET'S GHOST: Oh, thou incestuous, thou adulterate beast!

FALSTAFF: Gentlemen, gentlemen! For heaven's sake, keep order!

HAMLET'S GHOST: I was simply using Master Shakespeare's language; surely that's good enough for anybody.

CLAUDIUS: And I was merely expressing a wish which, had it been granted in time, would have prevented a terrible tragedy involving even my own life.

FALSTAFF: Yes, yes, gentlemen; but you forget there are ladies present.

LADY MACBETH: Oh, don't mind us; we are all married women.

MARIA: Yes, we can discriminate.

SIR TOBY: You bet!

FALSTAFF: Proceed with the roll call. What say you, Polonius?

POLONIUS: He made young Hamlet pretend that I was a rat, and kill me on the paltry wager of a dollar. Dead for a ducat, forsooth!

MACBETH: Hoot, mon! A ducat's a mickle o' money; it's a hundred bawbees.

SIR TOBY: It means oatmeal galore!

PISTOL: And muckle whiskey!

SHYLOCK: He robbed me of my ducats and my daughter; cheated me of my just revenge; deprived me of the prop that sustained my house, and made me cry content.

DOGBERRY: Yes, and he had me writ down an ass—me, a house-holder, an oficer, and, which is more, as pretty a piece of flesh as any is in Messina.

BOTTOM: He made a regular ass of me—me that can aggravate my voice, and roar you as gently as any sucking dove.

VERGES: And he had no suspect for my grey hairs.

LADY MACBETH: Of me, a woman of noble birth and gentle breeding, he made a whining somnambulist, wrestling with a damned spot, and enacting again the scene of a tragedy necessary to the honor and fame of Bonnie Scotland.

MRS. QUICKLY: Greatly against my grain and unnatural inclination, he wheedled me into making a false report of Sir John's death, and then married me to Pistol.

MERCUTIO: That was the most unkindest cut of all.

PISTOL: Sir!

FALSTAFF: But we have not heard from the noblest Roman of them all. What sayest thou, Antony?

ANTONY: I have no personal complaint, good Sir John. Shakespeare's treatment of Cleopatra and myself was very kind and considerate.

FALSTAFF: What, man! where is thy Roman pride? He served thee worse than Christopher Sly; he gave thee the first authenticated attack of delirium tremens.

ANTONY: Jest not, Sir John. It ill becomes the High Priest of Sack to speak lightly on such a theme.

FALSTAFF: I jest not, noble Antony, nor do I speak lightly. Bestir thy brains. Dost not recollect that scene with Eros? Didst thou not have "black vesper's pageants"? Didn't thou sometimes see a cloud that's dragonish, a vapor some time like a bear or a lion, a blue promontory with nodding trees upon 't, and green monkeys and pink rabbits that mocked and gibbered at thee?

ANTONY: Stop, I implore thee! Methinks I see them still!

PISTOL: He had them, sure enough!

ANTONY: I will take any pledge; I'll vote ay for anything.

FALSTAFF: Then are we all agreed and absolute for revenge. The next question is what form shall our vengeance take?

SHYLOCK: I move that Lady Macbeth, Dame Quickly, Maria, and our noble chairman be appointed a committee on that subject with power to act.

MERCUTIO: I cordially second that motion.

FALSTAFF: All in favor will say, Ay.

ALL: Ay!

FALSTAFF: Opposed? None! Is there any further business, gentlemen?

MERCUTIO: May I ask why there is such a small representation of female characters here?

FALSTAFF: An apposite question, very. Pistol, were the invitations extended to all our beloved sisters, without fear or favor?

PISTOL: Noble chairman, they were. Some of them were over timid to attend; some were fearful of coming to a tavern without male escorts. Ophelia, Desdemona and Viola made the excuse that they had nothing fit to wear. My lord Hamlet said that the constant dread of an insane asylum kept him in seclusion nowadays.

SIR TOBY: As there are some ladies present, and to avoid mishaps that might arise from that circumstance, I suggest that the convention bind itself to secrecy.

HAMLET'S GHOST: Swear!

FALSTAFF: That's the word, old truepenny; swear.

LADY MACBETH, MARIA, and **MRS. QUICKLY:** Oh, gentlemen, do not be so unkind; do not make us swear secrecy.

FALSTAFF: We must, we must, for the general safety.

SIR TOBY: Propose the oath, Sir John.

FALSTAFF: Swear, each and every one of you, upon my sword, the emblem of honor and true knighthood, that you will reveal to no one the proceedings of this day, so grace and mercy at your most need help you.

HAMLET'S GHOST: Swear!

CURTAIN.

ACT II

SCENE.–Shakespeare's Workshop. Three curtained cabinets labeled "Comedy," "History," "Tragedy." Armor and stage properties scattered around. Table with large paste-pot and shears, pens, ink, etc. Bookcase near table containing "Montaigne's Essays," North's "Plutarch," "Familiar Quotations," "Rhyming Dictionary," Abbott's "Shakespearian Grammar," etc.

[WILLIAM SHAKESPEARE *discovered at table.*]

SHAKESPEARE: To be or not to be? What an undying plague that question has become. It drops as easily from schoolboy's piping throat as from actor's tragic maw. It baffles the murky mind of melancholy, moonstruck youth, and distracts the aims of shaking, palsied eld. And what is't after all? A cheap catch-phrase rounded with the facile nib of a grey-goose quill; a perennial coil from the feathered membrane of a barnyard fowl! The wing of a goose the weapon of the wise. Foh! The conceit is sickening! It smells of Alexander and the beer barrel. But I must to work. [*Draws curtain of cabinet disclosing* OPHELIA *at a typewriter.*] Here's metal more attractive than a grey-goose quill! Art ready, sweet?

OPHELIA: I am, my lord.

SHAKESPEARE: My thanks are thine for that sweet word, Ophelia. A title of one's own is better far than a coat-of-arms for one's father. An it please thee, sweet one, I'll e'en rattle off a few lines for "The Tempest," which is billed for next week.

[OPHELIA *sits down with her note-book and writes as* SHAKESPEARE *dictates.*]

"You fools! I and my fellows are ministers of fate; the elements of whom your swords are tempered may as well wound the loud winds, or with bemocked-at stabs kill the still-closing waters, as diminish one dowle that's in my plume; my fellow ministers are alike invulnerable. If you could hurt, your swords are now too massy for your strengths, and will not be uplifted." Put that through thy typewriter sweet Ophelia, while I entrust Desdemona with a few gems of wingèd thought. [*Pulls curtain of next cabinet and discovers* DESDEMONA.]

Good-morrow, gentle Desdemona. Take thy graphite wand, I prithee, and let thy nimble digits transfix a verbal picture of my glowing thought. Where left we off last in "Measure for Measure"?

DESDEMONA: *[reading from notes]*. "Lucio (aside to Isabella): That's well said."

SHAKESPEARE: Ay, that's it.

DESDEMONA: *[writing]*. Who says that?

SHAKESPEARE: Says what, sweet?

DESDEMONA: "Ay, that's it."

SHAKESPEARE: Oh, strike that out, dear heart; that's not Shakespeare; that's a remark of my own. Nothing of my own must drift into the plays; 'twould be a deathblow to the learned commentators. Now proceed:

"Isabella: Could great men thunder as Jove himself does, Jove would ne'er be quiet, for every pelting, petty officer would use his heaven for thunder, nothing but thunder! Merciful heaven, thou rather with thy sharp and sulphurous bolt splitst the unwedgeable and gnarled oak than the soft myrtle; but man, proud man, drest in a little brief authority, most ignorant in what he is most assured, his glassy essence, like an angry ape, plays such fantastic tricks before high heaven as make the angels weep."

Pound away on that, gentle Desdemona, while I turn one of my sugared sonnets with Viola at the desk. *[Goes to next cabinet and discovers* VIOLA.*]* Take this fire-new from the mint, sweet Patience:

When in disgrace with fortune and men's eyes,
I all alone beweep my outcast state,
And trouble deaf heaven with my bootless cries,
And look upon myself, and curse my fate,
Wishing me like to one more rich in hope,
Featured like him, like him with friends possess'd,
Desiring this man's art, and that man's scope,
With what I most enjoy contented least:
Yet in these thoughts myself almost despising,
Haply I think on thee,—and then my state

(Like to the lark at break of day arising
From sullen earth) sings hymns at heaven's gate;
For thy sweet love remember'd, such wealth brings,
That then I scorn to change my state with kings.

OPHELIA: *[coming from cabinet with note-book].* How spell you "invulnerable," Master Shakespeare?

SHAKESPEARE: You can search me, Ophelia. Orthography and I are not on good terms. To flout the tricksy jade, I rarely spell my own name twice the same way. Spell it how it pleases thee, chuck, and risk it with the printers.

DESDEMONA: *[coming forward with note-book].* Oh, dear Master Shakespeare, in my notes there's a word I cannot decipher.

SHAKESPEARE: What looks it like, sweet?

DESDEMONA: Why, it might be almost anything, Master Shakespeare; magpie, martin, mouse or mortal—ah! that's it, "mortal";—"than the soft mortal."

SHAKESPEARE: Well, it matters not whate'er it be, swetheart; one word is as good as another in these benighted days. Let it be "mortal," an thou wilt, dear heart; some pedant will surely change it after it leaves the press, and pride himself on discovering a new reading. Let be, chuck, let be.

OPHELIA: That girl is abominable; she's always making excuses to hang around Will.

[Noise outside.]

SHAKESPEARE: By the twitching of my larboard ear, a harbinger of evil will now appear. To your eyries, my birds!

[Stenographers enter cabinets and draw the curtains. **SHAKESPEARE** *goes to table and assumes attitude of study. Enter* **BEN JONSON.***]*

JONSON: Look where my abridgement sits! I warrant there are tears in his eyes as well as distraction in his aspect. Ah! he writes. How swift the quill travels o'er the virgin sheet! No deletions, no carat marks, no pause for words. His brain throbbing with battalions of galloping thoughts, his eye in fine frenzy rolling, twisting the forms of things unknown into tangible shapes, and giving to airy nothing a local habitation and a name. What ho! my Shakespeare! Leave off thy damnable faces and greet thy friend.

SHAKESPEARE: *[throwing down pen]*. What! Ben Jonson, or I do forget myself.

JONSON: The same, friend Will, and thy poor servant ever.

SHAKESPEARE: I am very glad to see you. But what, in faith, bring you from the Mermaid, Ben?

JONSON: A sober disposition, Master Will.

SHAKESPEARE: I would not hear your enemy say so. I'll teach you to drink deeper ere you depart.

JONSON: An you do that, Will, I'll write a sonnet for the First Folio of thy plays, and fool the world with grand comparisons. But hast thou the wherewithal?

SHAKESPEARE: What! never say thou art thirsty, Ben.

JONSON: Thirsty! My lips are as dry as kippered herrings, and several bales of Sea Island cotton are lodged within my mouth!

SHAKESPEARE: A cup of ale is a dish for a king, eh, Ben?

JONSON: I prithee, do not mock me, fellow mummer. Even small ale is welcome in the morning. But where is it? Produce, Will, produce!

SHAKESPEARE: I am sorry for thy katzenjammer[6], Ben; but—

JONSON: What! another of thy tricks of fancy. Thou hast neither ale nor sack nor aqua vitæ. Thou art a villainous compound of frivolity and prevarication.

SHAKESPEARE: Say not so, good Ben. Why, I can call spirits from the vasty deep.

JONSON: Yes, I've heard that before. But will they come when thou dost call?

SHAKESPEARE: *[going to dumb-waiter, beckoning].* What see'st thou there?

[DESDEMONA, OPHELIA and VIOLA peep out of cabinets.]

JONSON: A fearful and dark abysm, rumbles of voices and odors pungent, powerful and pleasant. Heavens, Will, what mystery is this?

SHAKESPEARE: 'Tis my well of English undefiled! Now for an incantation. Stand back, Ben, stand back! *[Chants.]*

Black and White, Mountain Dew,
Come up quick for us two!

[Scotch whiskey, selzer bottle and glasses spring up. SHAKESPEARE *mixes two highballs, hands one to* JONSON, *who drinks and sighs in ecstasy.]*

JONSON: Day and night, this is wondrous strange!

SHAKESPEARE: Therefore, as a stranger, give it welcome, Ben.

JONSON: I will, I do! If this be magic, I'll make the most of it! Fill full again, Will.

[SHAKESPEARE mixes another drink for JONSON.]

Glorious, celestial, divine! How comes it hither?

SHAKESPEARE: That's one of the secrets of my art, Ben.

JONSON: I see; but, between ourselves, now—

SHAKESPEARE: Wilt keep the secret?

JONSON: As heaven is my judge, Will.

SHAKESPEARE: There's a spring in the well.

JONSON: A spring! Oh, ah! I see. Ha! ha! Well sprung, indeed!

SHAKESPEARE: Have another, Ben.

JONSON: Well, it's gratifying, and mighty searching; pleasing to the palate, and soothing to the pate. I must confess it likes me well. Yes, I think one more will do no harm, Will.

> [Drinks again, and SHAKESPEARE places the bottles back on the dumb-waiter, which descends quickly.]

> [Enter OTHELLO and MALVOLIO.]

MALVOLIO: We seek the honorable Master Shakespeare; which is he?

JONSON: Jumping Jupiter, the cross-gartered gull knows not his own father.

OTHELLO: Then you, I take it, are the great master.

JONSON: Now, what sane man would take me for Shakespeare? No, most honorable sootiness, there's your quarry. [Points to SHAKESPEARE.]

MALVOLIO: The heavens rain blessings on your honor.

OTHELLO: Excellent wretch, perdition catch my soul, but I do love thee, and when I love thee not, chaos is come again!

JONSON: What means this, Will? Canst thou not keep the puppets in order?

SHAKESPEARE: Of a truth, Ben, they sometimes get beyond me; but this is as strange to me as 'tis to thee. Now, my masters, be so good as to explain your presence here. I thought I had seen the last of ye!

MALVOLIO: I pray your honor to possess yourself in patience. We have matters of the gravest import to unfold.

OTHELLO: We would speak of plots dark and base, of intrigues foul and unnatural, of filial treachery and mutiny impious.

SHAKESPEARE and JONSON: Mutiny!

MALVOLIO: Ay, your worships, mutiny with its hideous train of blood and devastation. The pack is out and yelping for revenge.

SHAKESPEARE: Come, come, my friends, keep your bombast for the stage, and tell plainly what you mean.

MALVOLIO: Falstaff has escaped the Fleet, and hied himself to the Boar's Head.

SHAKESPEARE: Falstaff escaped! That's news, indeed! Tut! man, I'm afraid thy wit is still affected. Falstaff is dead; I killed him myself!

OTHELLO: Indeed, my lord, 'tis true. The measures you took for Sir John's demise were ineffectual. Dame Quickly was deceived thereby, and so were his comrades in drink and deviltry. But Falstaff is alive and well, and inflamed with designs of crimson vengeance. Robert Greene has been with him.

SHAKESPEARE: Death and damnation, O!

OTHELLO: Ah, I see you are moved. With cunning words and deep, Greene has turned the tide of filial affection against you. A meeting of your leading characters has been held with Falstaff in the chair. They have recounted their grievances against you. All are agreed upon retaliatory measures, and a committee is now devising what shape the punishment shall take.

SHAKESPEARE: *[faintly].* Lend me thy hand, Ben; my heart grows cold.

JONSON: Bear up, Will; cheerily, lad, cheerily. Don't show the white-feather in front of these mountebanks. May I ask, noble Othello, why you did not take part in this extraordinary convention?

OTHELLO: The knaves drew the color line on me. Otherwise I should have delivered a speech in opposition to the movement.

JONSON: Yes, you are fond of making speeches. On what ground would you have based your opposition?

OTHELLO: Sir, no fault have I to find with Master Shakespeare. My lines were always strong and mouth-filling, the situations were thrilling, and the end was bloody enough to satisfy my martial spirit.

JONSON: True, noble Othello; Will certainly showed kindness toward the colored race. 'Twas pity, though, the law against miscegenation was not enforced in your case.

OTHELLO: Toads and monkeys, sir!

JONSON: Don't get angry, noble Othello; that fustian doesn't count here. And you, Malvolio, why didn't you join the procession?

MALVOLIO: To be round with you, sir, 'twas because I had enemies in the convention.

JONSON: Ah, still governed by personal motives. Is that all you have to convey, gentlemen?

OTHELLO: We thought timely warning might enable Master Shakespeare to circumvent the mutinous rogues.

JONSON: Well, we are extremely obliged for your information, and now have the distinguished honor of bidding you good day. [Bows them to door, and returns to SHAKESPEARE.] Hearten thyself, Will. Forewarned is forearmed. There's time and to spare to foil the knaves.

SHAKESPEARE: 'Tis not that, Ben, not that that unmans me; 'tis the base ingratitude of my offspring. Think how I nursed them into public favor; the days and nights I toiled and moiled over them; the way in which I even begged, borrowed and stole to make them agreeable to popular taste. And Falstaff, of all my sprightly brood—for him to turn and rend me! It makes me sick at heart. Oh, Ben, 'tis sharper than a serpent's tooth to have a thankless child!

JONSON: Tush, man; away with mawky sentiment; rouse thy manly heart. We will to the Mermaid to devise swift means of punishment for this rebellious crew.

    [Exeunt.]

    [OPHELIA, DESDEMONA and VIOLA come from the cabinets.]

OPHELIA: Heard ye the fearful news, sisters?

VIOLA: It follows hard uon the mysterious hints that Pistol dropped.

DESDEMONA: My bosom swells with its terrible import.

VIOLA: 'Twas real nice of Othello to reveal the plot.

OPHELIA: 'Twas very unselfish on his part, seeing how fond he is of smothering things.

DESDEMONA: That's an unkind remark, Ophelia dear.

OPHELIA: Not unless you take it to yourself.

DESDEMONA: I had a Christian death-bed anyway, and not a suicide's grave.

OPHELIA: You horrid thing; no respectable Northern girl would have eloped with a Negro.

DESDEMONA: He was not a Negro; he was the Moor of Venice, and had royal blood in his veins. You're a nasty spiteful creature, and never had a husband at all.

VIOLA: Ladies! pray stop this wrangling; it's a serious reflection on our characters. Now, Ophelia, I am sure you meant no harm; and the gentle Desdemona is loved everywhere for her sweetness. Kiss and be friends.

> *[They embrace.]*

OPHELIA: Don't mind my horrible temper, dear.

DESDEMONA: 'Twas my fault; I'm sorry I was so unkind.

VIOLA: We must contrive means to aid Master Shakespeare in this crisis. What's best to be done?

OPHELIA: First, let's call comfort from his vasty deep.

DESDEMONA: Know you the spell?

OPHELIA: 'Tis as easy as lying. *[Goes to the dumb-waiter.]*

> Ice-cream and Ceylon tea,
> Send them up for us three!

[Dumb-waiter makes prompt delivery. Tea things are placed on table and OPHELIA *serves.]*

VIOLA: This reminds me of a picnic in Illyria.

DESDEMONA: It's better than a feast in Cyprus.

OPHELIA: Or a cold bath under a slanting willow tree.

VIOLA: It's invigorating.

DESDEMONA: And cheering.

OPHELIA: The nicest ever.

VIOLA: Of course, we must stick to Shakespeare.

OPHELIA: O, yes; what would we have been without him?

DESDEMONA: He certainly was good to me.

OPHELIA: Well, don't brag about it.

DESDEMONA: I was not bragging, dear Ophelia.

OPHELIA: Yes, you were.

DESDEMONA: I was not.

OPHELIA: Of course, you'll have the last word. You talked back with the pillow in your mouth.

DESDEMONA: It's a lie, a wicked lie!

OPHELIA: Don't you call me names, you common white trash!

VIOLA: Ladies, ladies! I beg of you not to quarrel. Think how it looks.

DESDEMONA: I am not quarreling; I'm too gentle to quarrel. *[Cries.]*

OPHELIA: *[crying]*. And I didn't mean anything. Kiss me again, sweet Desdemona.

[They embrace.]

VIOLA: Let's invoke the spirits in aid of Shakespeare.

DESDEMONA: That's a happy thought. But how shall we do't?

OPHELIA: You ought to know; you were wooed by witchcraft.

DESDEMONA: I was not; I was wooed and won by Othello's valor.

OPHELIA: Well, your father didn't believe that.

DESDEMONA: Don't you dare to say a word about my father.

OPHELIA: And why not, pray? Much you cared for your father when you ran off with a blackamoor.

DESDEMONA: Oh, I wish I were not so gentle; I'd scratch your horrid eyes out. No wonder Hamlet told you to go to a nunnery.

OPHELIA: Well, it's the last place one would find you in.

VIOLA: Ladies, ladies! how unseemly this is.

DESDEMONA: Marry come up, Miss Patience on a Monument! Mind your own business!

OPHELIA: Yes, do! You are entirely too meddlesome. You never told your love, you didn't, but you trapped the Duke all the same.

VIOLA: What I did was honorably done.

OPHELIA: No such thing! 'Twas unmaidenly done. You put on tights and masqueraded as a page.

DESDEMONA: And, pretending to be a man, you acted like a silly, giddy girl. I blushed for you when I heard of it.

VIOLA: Oh, why did I leave Illyria?

OPHELIA: Perhaps the Duke wearied of you.

VIOLA: Oh, oh!

DESDEMONA: There, there, don't cry, Viola. We are awfully wicked and spiteful.

OPHELIA: We are only women, you know.

VIOLA: You touched me on a tender spot, dear.

OPHELIA: Yes, I know. But let us forget and forgive, and never, never be naughty with one another again.

[They embrace.]

VIOLA: And now we'll call the spirits. I know how 'tis done; I watched Master Shakespeare when he was working on Macbeth. *[Goes to corner of room and brings forth a caldron.]* We must play the witches ourselves.

[They gather round the caldron.]

OPHELIA: Thrice the brinded cat hath mewed.

DESDEMONA: Thrice and once the hedge-pig whined.

VIOLA: Harpier cries, 'Tis time, 'tis time.

ALL: Black spirits and white; red spirits and grey;
   Mingle, mingle, mingle, you that mingle may.
   Titty, tiffin, keep it stiff in;
   Firedrake, Pucky, make it lucky;
   Liard, Robin, you must bob in.
   Round, around, around, about, about;
   All ill come running in; all good keep out.

[Thunder and lightning.]

VIOLA: Oh, they come, they come!

OPHELIA: I'm scared! oh!

[Thunder and lightning.]

DESDEMONA: Oh, oh!

[They hide in cabinets.]

[Enter FALSTAFF. Sniffs at caldron.]

FALSTAFF: What devil's instrument is this? No wonder I smelled brimstone. This must be the machine that makes his ghosts and goblins, his bearded witches and breechless fairies.

[OPHELIA *peeps out.*]

There's one now. They say that he speaks to them shall die. But that's a fable. I'll speak to it though it blast me. Stay illusion! If thou hast any sound or use of voice, speak to me.

OPHELIA: Why, it's old Jack Falstaff! Come, girls, here's nothing to be scared of.

[OPHELIA, DESDEMONA *and* VIOLA *surround* FALSTAFF.]

FALSTAFF: Bless my heart, here's three of them, and—yes—no, yes—it's that trinity of heroines in their stage attire. Here in Shakespeare's studio! I am pleased to meet ye, fair dames, but I mistrust your presence here. What a Turk that man must be!

OPHELIA: Do not impugn our motives, Sir John; we are here on business.

FALSTAFF: Business, forsooth; what business?

VIOLA: Our business.

DESDEMONA: And it's none of your business.

FALSTAFF: Well, judging from your variegated pasts, your business is of a nature that will not stand the test of critical examination.

OPHELIA: Good Sir John, be not so harsh with us. All flesh is frail.

FALSTAFF: No so, young woman, not so. Were all flesh frail, where would my morality be? 'Tis a false and foolish conclusion.

VIOLA: And do you, Sir John, set up as an example of virtue? When did you last see Master Ford, and how liked you the bath in Datchedmead?

FALSTAFF: Will that tale never be drowned? That's another score against Master Shakespeare. But I must dissemble. I know thy cunning, my pretty piece of painted propriety; thou played it nicely upon the beauteous Olivia. I wonder thou darest to show thy face in honest company. Hast no remorse or shame?

VIOLA: More than enough to save thee from Hades, were I so disposed, thou vile slanderer.

FALSTAFF: An you give me more of your tongue, I'll call the watch.

DESDEMONA: The watch, thou reeking bombard of sack and vanity; the watch would be only too glad to get hold of thy ugly carcase.

OPHELIA: Yea, verily; thy presence here causes a huge gap in the Fleet.

FALSTAFF: What a trio of viragoes! And but yesterday I thought them gentle, sweet and kind, like all that vagrant's heroines. Well, ladies, since soft words and mild persuasion avail naught, I shall call in Master Shakespeare's wife; perhaps she will have a few words to say to you.

ALL: Master Shakespeare's wife!

FALSTAFF: Ah, that strikes home! Yes, his wife, formerly Mistress Anne Hathaway, who has just arrived from Stratford to administer reproof and counsel to her recreant spouse.

OPHELIA: I won't believe it; the fat rogue is a notorious liar.

DESDEMONA: He seems in earnest; perhaps there is something behind this threat.

OPHELIA: Misgivings seize me also. Oh, these men, these men!

FALSTAFF: It takes, it takes! The knave has been trifling with their young affections.

VIOLA: *[after wispering with the others]*. Good Sir John, tell us it is not so; say you said it to tease us.

FALSTAFF: So that's the way the land lays, is it? That's why you flouted my messengers. You had nothing to wear, eh? It seems to me you have it on, Mistress Viola, and very becoming, too, with your lovely figure.

VIOLA: Oh, you ill-mannered wretch!

DESDEMONA: Would that Othello were here now!

FALSTAFF: Would he were, pillows and all!

OPHELIA: You are an unfeeling ruffian!

VIOLA: A footpad and a bully!

DESDEMONA: A common thief, a runagate!

OPHELIA: A besotted, lying, scoundrelly rake!

VIOLA: Let's scratch his eyes out!

[They dash at FALSTAFF, who runs out crying, "Mistress Shakespeare, Mistress Shakespeare."]

[Enter SHAKESPEARE.]

SHAKESPEARE: What ails ye, girls?

ALL: Falstaff!

SHAKESPEARE: Falstaff!

OPHELIA: Ay, that muddy, corpulent knight-errant of thine.

SHAKESPEARE: How came he hither?

DESDEMONA: We were calling upon the spirits to preserve thee, and lo! Falstaff appeared!

SHAKESPEARE: So ye were meddling with my magic art! How oft have I warned ye to beware of curiosity, the emerald-hued enemy of your sex that grows by what it feeds upon. But there's no obedience or fealty in woman! Would that the devil had come in answer to your spells!

VIOLA: You are very rude, Master Shakespeare!

DESDEMONA: And cruel and unkind!

OPHELIA: And a low, deceitful married man!

VIOLA: And we just hate you, we do!

[They weep.]

SHAKESPEARE: Merciful powers! They know my secret!

DESDEMONA: And we were so happy and trustful!

OPHELIA: Devoted to his service!

VIOLA: And loyal to his dearest aims!

[They weep again.]

SHAKESPEARE: This ecstasy amazes me! How have I been cruel, or unkind, or deceitful? Ye were ever the children of my happiest fancy, the fairy forms of my divinest love, the apples of my impassioned eyes! The dark lady of my sonnets was not so dear to my heart; and yet, in one brief moment, I find ye changed to furies tearing passion to tatters in senseless rage. Say, why is this?

OPHELIA: Then, 'tis not true; you are not a married man?

SHAKESPEARE: Do I look like a married man?

DESDEMONA: He equivocates.

VIOLA: He speaks not by the card.

OPHELIA: And betrays us all.

[They weep.]

SHAKESPEARE: By heaven, I swear—

[Enter FALSTAFF, leading MRS. QUICKLY, disguised as MISTRESS SHAKESPEARE.]

FALSTAFF: Don't be alarmed, my dear Mistress Shakespeare; I'll be bound this is not the only time you have heard him swear. Take a good look around before you embrace your loving husband. Note what company he keeps—two grass widows and an adventuress from Elsinore.

MRS. QUICKLY: Oh, you brazen trulls! What are you doing with my husband?

VIOLA: We are no trulls, I'd have you know, Madam; we are Master Shakespeare's stenographers.

MRS. QUICKLY: Stenographers! Oh, good Sir John, listen to that! Stenographers! Could it be worse, Sir John, could it be worse? I have heard of these stenographers! They lisp and they amble and murder the Queen's English; and go to the playhouse with their masters, and eat up our substance at tavern lunches, while doting wives sit lonesomely miserable at home! Stenographers! Oh, my fan and my salts, Sir John; I am quite flustrated with agitating commotions.

FALSTAFF: Be calm. Mistress Shakespeare, be calm. Appearances are certainly against him, but he may still be true, he may still be true!

MRS. QUICKLY: Oh, dear Sir John, look at the man, and then tell me he stays in London for nothing but play-acting, while I sit at home darning and spinning and worriting to make ends meet. Look at him, quite chapfallen, dumbfounded as a mouse in the paws of a cat.

FALSTAFF: Now that I mark him, he has a hangdog expression. For shame, Master Shakespeare! Dismiss these trulls! Take the wife of your youth to your bosom. Ask her pardon like a man.

SHAKESPEARE: Sir John Falstaff, 'twas not long ago that I loved thee. I glossed over thy faults and thy follies with tender hand. Against my better judgment I persuaded myself that thy heart was as big as thy bulk, and that thy multitude of sins evaporated in beams of good nature and fecundity of wit. Now do I see that I was wrong. Thou hast abused my charity, decried my fair fame, and maliciously disturbed my peace. And now, to cap all, thou bringest this foolish woman to masquerade as my wife, when thou knowest full well that I am free of the bonds of matrimony and slave to no woman on earth.

FALSTAFF: 'Tis false; thou'rt married; here is the ocular proof!

MRS. QUICKLY: Dost thou wrong me first and deny me afterward? O woeful day! My poor children! Take me back to Stratford, Sir John, and there let me die!

VIOLA: Master Shakespeare, we are really and truly sorry for you; but if this woman is your lawful wife, we will forgive the harsh words she has applied to us, and beg that you will be reconciled to her.

OPHELIA: Our hearts may break, but we will depart content an you kiss and make up with her.

DESDEMONA: See how the poor lady suffers from your coldness. Take her to your bosom, Master Shakespeare.

FALSTAFF: There's self-denial for you! There's Christian good-will and self-abnegation! Ladies, I salute you. You are pure and unadulterated ornaments of your sex!

MRS. QUICKLY: I will never speak ill of stenographers again. Come and buss me, Will.

> *[She approaches* **SHAKESPEARE** *with outstretched arms.* **SHAKESPEARE** *repulses her.* **FALSTAFF** *goes to door and beckons. Other characters troop in and form picture.]*

FALSTAFF: Friends, Romans, citizens, lend me your ears! You all have occasion to know William Shakespeare. To some of you he has been cruel where he should have been kind. Most of you owe him a grudge for indignities received at his hands. He has dealt with you often, not according to your just deserts, or according to the strict canons of dramatic law, but simply as his changeful mood guided him, now in sorrow, now in anger, sometimes in mad rage, and again with diabolical spleen and sardonic spite. He now stands exposed to all posterity as a common trickster. Mark him well. The giglot fortune no longer befriends him. The star of his destiny growns dim and obscure. For to-day, friends and compatriots, Master Shakespeare falls flat from his pedestal, and grovels in the dust as a vulgar married man. There stands his trustful wife, new-lighted from Stratford-on-Avon, with the love-light in her eyes and the ecstasy of passion in her swelling stomacher. Kiss him, sweet Mistress Shakespeare; and joy to Shakespeare, the married man!

[MRS. QUICKLY throws her arms around SHAKESPEARE'S *neck; he throws her off.]*

SHAKESPEARE: I tell you this woman is not my wife.

ALL: Shame, shame!

FALSTAFF: We may now leave him to the sweets of reconstructed matrimony.

ALL: Hail! Shakespeare, the married man!

CURTAIN.

ACT III

SCENE.—*Courtyard of Boar's Head Tavern.*

[One or two loungers on benches; OSTLERS *going to and fro;* FALSTAFF *enters from the tavern, looking glum and discontented.]*

FALSTAFF: The game doesn't go as merrily as it might. The surprise party was a success as far as it went, but Quickly's part therein seems to have disgruntled my erstwhile loyal ancient. He looks at everything with a parsimonious eye; he is suspiciously inquisitive as to my financial prospects, and somewhat dubious about my intercourse with his wife. And then there is a plot brewing. I hear whispers about returning loyalty to Shakespeare. I must be bold and resolute. My personal comfort demands better treatment than I am rewarded with. There is no other course. That bombastic tyke, Pistol, must stand aside. His spouse must be divorced. I must again be monarch of all I survey. Francis!

FRANCIS: *[within].* Anon, anon, sir.

FALSTAFF: Bid Mistress Quickly attend me here.

[Enter MRS. QUICKLY.*]*

MRS. QUICKLY: Pistol says time is precious as money, Sir John.

FALSTAFF: Both were made for slaves, good dame. I have sent for thee, sweet Quickly, because I owe thee much.

MRS. QUICKLY: Forty pounds, Sir John, not counting to-day's score.

FALSTAFF: Nay, that follows not, sweet hostess.

MRS. QUICKLY: Indeed, and it does, Sir John; Pistol says not a cup of sack but must go on the slate.

FALSTAFF: Tush, woman! I speak not of scores or of sack. On nobler themes my thoughts are bent.

MRS. QUICKLY: Pray God they do not break us, Sir John.

FALSTAFF: Hast thou no poetry in thy soul, dame? Forget thy pols and edipols for a while, and listen with ears intent.

MRS. QUICKLY: La! Sir John, you frighten me, indeed thou dost. 'Twas thus you looked and spoke when you were ill of that burning quotidian tertian. Let me call the leech; do, Sir John, there's a good man.

FALSTAFF: Heaven grant me patience!

MRS. QUICKLY: Oh, oh, Sir John, thou'rt ill, I am sure; but I hope there's no need of troubling about heaven yet. I am so worried that every part about me is quivering. And it's just about the turning o' the tide!

FALSTAFF: Peace, good woman, peace. Try to understand me. I tell thee again, in tones that should carry full conviction, that I owe thee much.

[MRS. QUICKLY makes sign of interrupting.]

Woman, at thy peril interrupt my soliloquy again! Within this wall of flesh, gentle Quickly, there is a soul that counts thee her creditor, and with advantage means to pay thy love.

MRS. QUICKLY: *[turning to go].* I'll bring the score, Sir John; Pistol said thou must settle when thou hadst means to pay.

FALSTAFF: Great Goliath's grandmother! Was ever man crossed so before? I must descend to her level, or these artless digressions will undo me quite. Mrs. Quickly, hear me for my cause, and be silent that thou mayst hear. I love thee, Quickly, I love thee.

MRS. QUICKLY: Oh, Sir John, Sir John!

FALSTAFF: Not with the faltering, sickly, sentimental affection of a purposeless youth, but with the fiery martial ardor of a tried and true knight, whose one aim and end shall be to shelter thee in his bosom and shield thy shrinking beauty from the storms and tempests of this rough world. Mrs. Quickly, Helena, Nell! On my knees I beg thee to listen to the voice of my true loving heart.

[Starts to kneel, but thinks better of it.]

MRS. QUICKLY: *[in confusion].* Oh, do not kneel, Sir John; rise, I pray you. What if Pistol saw you?

FALSTAFF: Pistol! A fig for Pistol. He is a very serpent in my way! I'll grind him to dust beneath my heel!

MRS. QUICKLY: Oh, thou honeysuckle villain! Wouldst thou kill my husband?

FALSTAFF: Ay, twenty such husbands an they stand between me and thy sweet love.

MRS. QUICKLY: Oh, here's bigamy and treason at work; here's foul conspiracy and murder. Help, Pistol, help! Bring a rescue!

FALSTAFF: Zounds, woman, hold thy peace: thou'lt affright the tavern.

MRS. QUICKLY: Oh, thou honey-seed rogue, thou man queller and woman queller. This comes of nursing a viper! Pistol! Good Pistol, bring some rescues!

[Enter NYM, BARDOLPH, and PISTOL.]

PISTOL: How now? Whose mare is dead?

[MRS. QUICKLY falls upon his neck, weeping.]

MRS. QUICKLY: Oh, Pistol, Pistol! Am I not thy true and wedded wife?

PISTOL: Ay, as fast as bell, book and candle can make thee!

MRS. QUICKLY: He assails my honor with centurion breath; he prates of beggarly divorcement; he swears he will crush thee with his venomous foot. Oh, Pistol, Pistol!

PISTOL: [releasing himself and facing FALSTAFF with hand on sword]. These be humors, indeed! What! shall we have incisions, shall we imbrue?

FALSTAFF: [drawing]. Away, you scullion! I'll tickle your catastrophe!

PISTOL: [drawing]. Ah! Have we not Hiren[7] here? [Aside to NYM and BARDOLPH.] Gather round me, lambkins.

[They draw in his support.]

Down climbing pride to Stygian Tartary. Let grievous, ghastly, gaping wounds untwine the sisters three! Come, Atropos, come!

MRS. QUICKLY: Alas! alas! put up your naked weapons, put up your naked weapons!

BARDOLPH: Strike to his heart!

NYM: Slash off his caitiff head!

[All three fence with FALSTAFF and drive him out.]

PISTOL: *[sheathing sword].* A rascal bragging slave! he fled from me like quicksilver.

MRS. QUICKLY: *[embracing him].* Ah, you valiant little villain!

[FALSTAFF appears at door crying, "All hell shall stir for this!" They rush toward him and he flees.]

PISTOL: Let's within, lads, and celebrate this glorious victory!

[Exeunt.]

[Enter SHAKESPEARE and JONSON.]

SHAKESPEARE: This tavern has a pleasant seat; the odors nimbly and sweetly recommend themselves unto our gentler senses.

JONSON: The bird of summer, the beer-loving hobo, does approve by his loved attendance, that the bottle's breath smells wooingly here. Where he most drinks and haunts, I have observed, the odors are always delicate.

SHAKESPEARE:
Then is he ev'rywhere. All the world's a tavern,
And all the men and women merely drinkers;
They have their cocktails and their whiskey straight,
And one man in his time drinks many quarts,
His course being seven stages. At first a clear head,
Sober and steadfast in all good resolves;
Then the morning bitters, with cherry red
Or slice of mellow pine, creeping like snail,
Unwillingly to toil. And then the tippler,
Sneaking back again, with a woeful story
Of pains internally. Then a toper,
Full of strange oaths and loaded to the guard,

Jealous in potting, eager, and quick to imbibe,
Seeking the bubbling repetition
Even at the bottle's mouth. And then the drunkard,
With grumbling belly with poor liquor lined.
With eyes bleary and beard for days uncut,
Foolish in speech and prone to quarreling;
And so he swills his part. The sixth stage shifts
Into the grim and ragged runagate,
With carbuncles on nose and patch on head,
His bloated face begrimed, while bar to bar
He beats his way; and his big manly voice,
Unhinged by rum and thirst colossal, pleads
And whimpers for a drink. Last scene of all,
That ends this sad and shameful history,
Is beastly sottishness and foul oblivion—
Sans soul, sans sense, sans hope, sans everything!

JONSON: Gracious, Will, what a temperance lecturer thou'dst make, an thou swore off and reformed!

SHAKESPEARE: True temperance, Ben, is not total abstinence; it uses well the gifts the gods bestow; it accepts good wine as a trusty servant, not as a tyrannic slave-master; and in that respect, temperance is man's finest grace and virtue.

JONSON: Art thou fully reconciled to Sir Toby's plot to put down Falstaff?

SHAKESPEARE: 'Tis meet he had a lesson; they say he is puff'd up with his last exploit, and is belording it o'er his fellows. So long as the project results in no serious hurt—for I confess I love the rogue despite his vanity and bibulous conceit—I am in favor of it.

JONSON: Danger is remote, while the outcome may be wholesome in many respects. To hoodwink the watch, we'll have to dub the match a test of two rival schools of physical culture.

SHAKESPEARE: Ah! a practical exposition of the respective merits of sack and tobacco in the development of physical man.

JONSON: Precisely so; an object lesson of the utmost value to the rising generation.

SHAKESPEARE: But art sure thy man will come to the scratch? 'Tis said he is an arrant coward and boaster.

JONSON: What, Bobadil! You'd have no doubts if you heard him talk. With nineteen men as skilled in the weapon as himself, he will undertake to slaughter an army of forty thousand men in two hundred days; that is twenty men each, day in and day out, without counting time lost in sleep and harmless recreation.

SHAKESPEARE: Good heavens, Ben; that makes him a worse fire-eater than Falstaff.

JONSON: You will find him sowhen you see him at work. But how about your man? I've heard said that he kills nothing but dead men.

SHAKESPEARE: That's a base libel. He has been known to engage eleven men in buckram at once, alone and single handed, and kill seven of them before he was winded.

JONSON: Then it's pretty near an even match. We'll about it at once. Sir Toby has Captain Bobadil in training, and he'll be here anon. We must get Falstaff in trim. What ho, mine host Pistol!

[Enter PISTOL*.]*

SHAKESPEARE: Where lies Sir John Falstaff, Pistol?

PISTOL: In sulphurous pit with fiends grim and damned.

SHAKESPEARE: That's news indeed. When left he these lodgings?

PISTOL: My spouse he envied, and forth with flashing sword I drove him. Under the ribs I jerked him thrice, and thrice I pierced his bread-basket. His quietus he has got.

JONSON: It seems we are too late, Will.

SHAKESPEARE: This fellow's bark is always worse than his bite. He thrives on extravagant phrases. I warrant Falstaff is safe and sound enough. Hark ye, mine host Pistol; a word in your ear, sirrah!

*[*PISTOL *approaches and* SHAKESPEARE *whispers to him.]*

PISTOL: Your wish is law. The braggart vile I'll find and fetch him straight. What ho, lambkins, appear!

[Enter NYM *and* BARDOLPH.*]*

JONSON: Lambkins! He meant scarecrows!

PISTOL: Look that your irons be trim; work hot and bloody lies before us. Attention, lads! March!

[They march out with swords drawn, PISTOL *leading.]*

SHAKESPEARE: Poor old Jack! He's been up to his old tricks! Wine and women will be his ruin.

JONSON: In part, thou art to blame for it, Will. What's bred in the bone will come out in the flesh. But see where my champion comes!

[Enter SIR TOBY *and* CAPTAIN BOBADIL, *the latter smoking a cigarette.]*

SIR TOBY: Thus far have we marched into the enemy's country without impediment, barring hesitation on the part of the bold captain's legs. At times I thought he had locomotor ataxia from smoking this same filthy, roguish tobacco.

JONSON: He hath a natural hesitancy in his walk, Sir Toby. How dost thou, brave captain?

BOBADIL: By the foot of Pharaoh, never better, Master Jonson.

JONSON: I would borrow thy ear for a moment.

*[*BOBADIL *and* JONSON *confer apart.]*

SHAKESPEARE: What of the captain, Toby; will he hold?

SIR TOBY: There's not enough blood in his liver to clog the foot of a flea. Falstaff will eat him, boots and all.

SHAKESPEARE: Well, keep his courage at the sticking place.

SIR TOBY: Never fear me, Master Will.

[Enter PISTOL, *followed by* NYM *and* BARDOLPH *carrying* FALSTAFF *on a stretcher.]*

PISTOL: Set down the carcase.

[They put down the stretcher.]

BOBADIL: What, is the brave knight dead?

SIR TOBY: *[who has been examining the body].* No, he's hot-scotched, not killed!

PISTOL: True, Sir Toby; we found him catching high-balls in the tenderloin; one struck him in the midriff, and over he keeled. He'll wake again to-morrow.

JONSON: To-morrow! He must wake to-night. Mañanas were banned by chieftain Macbeth, whose hot-scotch yesterdays lighted fools to death.

SHAKESPEARE: Give him a hypodermic injection of sack.

*[*BARDOLPH *brings bucket and half-gallon syringe.* SIR TOBY *charges the syringe and jabs the point into* FALSTAFF'S *arm.* FALSTAFF *groans and sighs.]*

A few drams more.

SIR TOBY: It must be in the other arm, then; this one will hold no more.

[Operation repeated on the other arm. FALSTAFF *raises himself to a sitting posture.]*

FALSTAFF: Give me a cup of sack! Bind up my wounds! Falstaff's himself again! *[Struggles to his feet.]* Soft! Did I but dream? What means this ghastly company? *[Rubs his eyes.]* I see them still, and on their faces looks that bode no good. Avaunt and quit my sight! Let the earth hide ye! Your bones are marrowless, your blood is cold; there is no speculation in those eyes with which ye glare!

BOBADIL: Alas! poor knight, he is mad!

SIR TOBY: He could be touched for the evil.

PISTOL: 'Twould be useless, Sir Toby; he never has a groat!

JONSON: Bi-chloride of gold is the only cure.

PISTOL: Not in this house, Master Jonson; this is no Keeley institute.[8]

SHAKESPEARE: He wants something to shake his shaking. Give him a cup of sack.

BARDOLPH: Yea, a hair of the dog that bit him.

BOBADIL: [producing tobacco]. Try some of this Trinidado, Sir John. It's a royal remedy for rabies. It is an antidote against sack and aqua vitæ. For the expulsion of tremors, crudities and obstructions, it has no equal on God's green earth.

FALSTAFF: Now, by heaven, my blood begins my safer guides to rule. Now do I know ye all! You and you, sirs [to SHAKESPEARE and JONSON], are miserable, canting ballad-mongers; you [to SIR TOBY] are a common midnight reveler; you [to PISTOL, NYM, and BARDOLPH] are sneaks and coystrills, detestable slanders of the heroic age in which ye live; and you [to BOBADIL], Sir Lantern-jaw, are a hypocritical, lying agent of the American Tobacco Trust.

SHAKESPEARE: Bravo, Sir John; that is the affront direct.

JONSON: [to BOBADIL]. Give him back the lie!

BOBADIL: But he is such a huge man.

JONSON: Therefore the easier to hit. Zounds, man, answer him in kind.

BOBADIL: Pardon me, Sir John, but you are entirely mistaken.

SIR TOBY: [prodding him in the ribs]. A little more ginger, captain.

BOBADIL: By Hercules, I do hold it, and will hold it before any knight in Christendom, that tobacco is the most sovereign and precious weed that ever nature tendered to the use of man.

FALSTAFF: And I say you lie, you rogue! Tobacco is not in it with sack. Sack drives all crude and foolish notions from the brain, and fills it with nimble, fiery and delectable shapes. It warms the blood and reddens the face. It stirs the heart to any deed of courage. It is the backbone of all valor, the core of all enterprises of pith and moment. In its operations it is twice blest; it blesseth him that gives and him that takes. 'Tis mightiest in the merriest, and enthrills the throned monarch better than his crown. All this and more will I with bright sword maintain against any tobacco-smoking knave in Christendom.

SHAKESPEARE: Bravo, bravo!

BOBADIL: Must I answer him again? He seems bold with rage.

SIR TOBY: Ay, challenge him to mortal combat. Never shake, man. He'd rather drink than fight.

BOBADIL: Rude, blustering knight, there I throw my gage. *[Throws down cigarette box.]* If sherris-sack hath left thee so much strength as to take up my honor's pawn, then stoop. I will make good against thee, arm to arm, what I have spoke, or thou canst worse devise.

> *[FALSTAFF tries to pick up the box and fails; PISTOL gets it and hands it to him.]*

FALSTAFF: I have ta'en it up by proxy, but with my own arm, good and true, I'll prove thee false to manhood, to physical development untrue, and a double-dyed traitor to the liquor dealers' association.

JONSON: *[to SHAKESPEARE].* Only blood can wipe out this defy.

SHAKESPEARE: *[to PISTOL].* Prepare the lists at once, and herald abroad news of the tournament.

> *[Stage is prepared. Other characters come in; FALSTAFF is made ready by BARDOLPH; SIR TOBY acts as second to BOBADIL.]*

JONSON: Good friends, the combat you are about to behold will solve for all time the comparative merits of sack and tobacco. Here stands Captain Bobadil, the doughty champion of the fragrant weed, to prove by his prowess that all the virtues that ennoble mankind are the product of tobacco.

SHAKESPEARE: And here, good friends, standeth Sir John Falstaff, the colossal man of war, on pain to be found false and recreant, to approve by his courage and skill that tobacco is a filthy, noxious weed, and that the world's salvation lies in sherris-sack.

PISTOL: Sound trumpets and set forward combatants!

> *[*BOBADIL *and* FALSTAFF *face each other as the trumpets blare; they feint a while and retreat in confusion.]*

FALSTAFF: I cannot fight with such a forked radish; there's not enough of him to hit.

BOBADIL: The contest is certainly unequal. Why, he turns the scales at three hundred and fifty pounds.

JONSON: There's no help for it now; the fight must on!

SHAKESPEARE: Fear not, Sir John; you shall do well enough.

PISTOL: He lacketh a cup of sack. No man can fight on a dry stomach.

> *[*FRANCIS *takes wine to* FALSTAFF.*]*

SIR TOBY: Lackest thou anything, captain? Would'st drink some tobacco?

BOBADIL: Methinks it would be good for my nerves.

> *[*SIR TOBY *gives him a cigarette, which he lights.]*

FALSTAFF: *[drinking].* Ah! nectar divine! great breeder of pluck!

BOBADIL: *[smoking].* Ah! Odor seraphic, grand master of brain and heart!

FALSTAFF: I'll wipe thee from the face of the earth!

SIR TOBY: *[to* BOBADIL*].* Have at him with a downright blow.

> *[They feint again and retreat in confusion.]*

FALSTAFF: I cry appeal; this contest is contrary to all the approved rules of chivalry.

JONSON: Tut! man, thou'rt afraid.

SHAKESPEARE: Patience, Ben; let's hear the plaint.

FALSTAFF: This forked radish must either come up to my weight, or I must get down to his; otherwise the match is off according to Hoyle.

SIR TOBY: Now's your time, Bobby lad; bluff, bluff for all thou'rt worth, and the fight is thine.

BOBADIL: May it please your honors, the knight makes an impossible demand. But there is a way out. Let my dimensions, against which the knight protests, be chalked upon his own portly person, and let all blows outside those lines be counted foul.

ALL: Hurrah for Bobadil!

SIR TOBY: How say you, Sir John; do you agree?

FALSTAFF: It sounds reasonable enough, but I'd rather you'd twine his anatomy round the circumference of a beer-barrel conforming to my size, and then I'll be at him hammer and tongs.

ALL: Hurrah for Falstaff!

SHAKESPEARE: Leave it to the seconds.

JONSON: Agreed.

> [PISTOL and SIR TOBY consult; then BARDOLPH takes the dimensions of BOBADIL and outlines them in chalk on FALSTAFF. FALSTAFF and BOBADIL then feint again and retreat as before.]

FALSTAFF: The clock! I must have the clock. I only fight by Shrewsbury clock!

> [Clock labeled "Shrewsbury" brought forward, and they confront each other again.]

SHAKESPEARE: [to FALSTAFF]. An thou balk again, I'll have Pistol run thee through.

SIR TOBY: [to BOBADIL]. If thou fallest back again, it will be upon the point of my sword.

[They now fight fiercely, the characters crying "Bravo, sack," "Bravo, tobacco!" **BOBADIL'S** *sword jabs* **FALSTAFF'S** *side three inches outside the chalk line, and* **FALSTAFF** *drops to the ground.]*

ALL: Tobacco wins!

SHAKESPEARE: 'Twas a foul.

JONSON: Not so, Master Shakespeare. The stroke was fair and fetching. According to the code adopted, your man is not hurt. Bobadil has simply let his wind out.

PISTOL: Then he's done for; wind was his stock-in-trade!

*[***FALSTAFF*** *staggers to his feet, approaches* **SHAKESPEARE,** *and falls.]*

FALSTAFF: Thy pardon I crave, Will. This unlooked-for stroke, while it ruins my bodily life, clears my spiritual vision. At last I see the grievous error of my ways. Serpents, sirens and sack have been my downfall. I prithee, Sweet Will, forgive me. My breath comes with difficulty; my heart scarce beats; my eyes grow dim. Call Dame Quickly to me.

*[***MRS. QUICKLY*** *goes and ministers to him.]*

Ah! at last I rest on thy bosom, sweet Nell. See the buttercups and daisies! Flowers are my playmates, Nell. There's rosemary for thee; that's for remembrance. There's pansies *[to* **PISTOL***]*; that's for thoughts.

JONSON: Thoughts and remembrance fitted; a document in grief.

FALSTAFF: Put more clothes on my feet, Nell. The sun hides its face, and the wind moans sadly in the waving corn. See! there is Herne, the hunter! Cheerily, cheerily, cheerily sounds the horn. The meadows are green and restful. Ah! the summer fields, the—green—green—summer fields! *[Dies.]*

JONSON: Alas, poor Jack!

SHAKESPEARE: Farewell, old comrade! We could have better spared a better man!

MRS. QUICKLY: Oh, he must not part like this. Poor Sir John.

SIR TOBY: Don't give up hope; we may be deceived again.

MRS. QUICKLY: Yes, yes! we may all be perceived once more. Bring a mirror and a feather, good Pistol. *[PISTOL gives her a large ostrich feather, which she places to* **FALSTAFF'S** *mouth.]* Dear, dear! It does not stir! The mirror, Pistol, the mirror! *[PISTOL gives her a mirror, and she holds it to his lips.]* Not a breath, not a cipher! Oh, he is dead and gone, dead and gone!

BARDOLPH: Nil desperandum! Never say die!

NYM: That's the humor of it!

SIR TOBY: There's only on more test; if that fails, he is dead, indeed. Bring a cup of sack, Francis!

> *[The wine is brought and* **SIR TOBY** *places the cup to* **FALSTAFF'S** *lips.* **FALSTAFF** *sighs, opens his eyes, seizes the cup and drinks.]*

SHAKESPEARE: Called back by sack! The rogue will never die while there's liquor in England.

> *[***FALSTAFF***, meantime, has risen and takes C. of stage.]*

FALSTAFF: What! you thought old Jack was dead? Never fear for me! Ye cannot kill Falstaff. I'll live forever, if only to show that good liquor and a merry heart are the panaceas for all the ills that flesh is heir to. Francis, a cup of sack! you rogue!

FRANCIS: Anon, anon, sir!

CURTAIN.

RE-TAMING OF THE SHREW
A Shakespearean Travesty

IN ONE ACT

BY

JOHN W. POSTGATE

CHARACTERS.

PETRUCHIO—*A Mad-cap Ruffian Tamed by Marriage*
ANGELO—*Stern Magistrate Softened by Matrimony*
DUKE OF ILLYRIA—*Sentimental Lover Turned Meek Husband*
OTHELLO—*Fierce Black General Under Sway of his Wife*
MACBETH—*Scottish Chieftain Fond of "the Barley Bree"*
GRUMIO—*Reformed Servant of Petruchio*
KATHERINE—*Leader in Woman's Rights Movement*
MARIANA—*Formerly Despondent Lady of the Moated Grange*
VIOLA—*Patience on a Monument Prior to her Marriage*
DESDEMONA—*Becomes Suffragist after Eloping with the Moor*
LADY MACBETH—*Strong-minded, Caustic Wife of Witch-ridden Macbeth*

TIME OF PLAYING—*About Forty-five Minutes.*

STORY OF THE PLAY.

After her woeful honeymoon, Katherine becomes an ardent suffragist and imposes household duties on Petruchio, who submits tamely to petticoat government. At a meeting of the women, man's doom as a political or domestic power is announced, but Katherine, Mariana, Viola, Desdemona and Lady Macbeth hark back to the past and twit one another on exciting episodes in their respective careers. They are on the verge of a quarrel several times, but kiss and make up and begin all over again.

This sisterhood of sweet, sympathetic souls determines to be true and loyal to the suffrage cause and compel the submission of their husbands. Before they leave for the club-house Katherine gives Petruchio permission to invite a few friends for a quiet evening. She instructs Grumio to serve nothing but barley water and to see that his master goes to bed at ten o'clock. Before his guests arrive, Petruchio tries in vain to have something stronger substituted for this insipid beverage. Macbeth, who is the first to appear, is delighted with the prospect of a gaudy night. He imagines that the bowl is filled with barley bree, his favorite tipple. As the others come in there is hearty greeting all round which, however, turns to dismay when the cups are charged and tasted. Grumio is sent out for stronger ingredients, and returns with turpentine, furniture polish, cider, grape juice, pepper pods, etc., which are emptied into the bowl.

This mixture gives great satisfaction. It has both fire and grip, and the erstwhile meek husbands soon become groggy, musical and courageous. While they are roaring "Auld Lang Syne," the ladies return from the club. Katherine is indignant at the scene presented, but she is met with bold and cutting remarks that presage male insurrection. Indeed, the strange liquor has done its work too well. Each and every one of the men, formerly so docile and obedient, defy their wives. Two hostile camps are at once formed. The women find it politic to abandon part of the ground already won in this battle for freedom. The men insist upon a restoration of their ancient rights and privileges. It is not until an appeal to the divorce court is threatened that the women acknowledge defeat. Then there is a season of reconciliation and the married couples depart apparently content and happy.

Katherine hands her big baby, Petruchio, the nursing bottle filled with "soothing syrup," Petruchio soothes her with a loving kiss, and the curtain falls on this timely travesty, which is replete with Shakespearean humor adapted to modern situations.

CHARACTERS AND COSTUMES.

This travesty draws material from five plays of Shakespeare—"Taming of the Shrew," "Measure for Measure," "Twelfth Night," "Othello" and "Macbeth." Where the services of a theatrical costumer are available, the characters may be dressed in accordance with the demands of the regular stage. A good effect may be gained, however, by modernizing the costumes. The following suggestions are offered for an effective color scheme:

PETRUCHIO—Old shooting jacket, knickerbockers and top-boots; military mustache and imperial; low-necked collar with flowing tie.

ANGELO—Black clothes and silk stockings; smooth shaven face, eyeglasses and judicial wig.

OTHELLO—Military costume, with cloak; black face.

MACBETH—Highland costume, including kilt and tartan.

GRUMIO—Rough doublet with belt at waist; trunks and coarse hose; smooth face.

DESDEMONA—Long, loose cream-colored gown with flowing sleeves; a small, round cap of gold or embroidery and violet scarf draped loosely round the waist and knotted in front.

KATHERINE—Green over-dress with pointed bodice; skirt and waist open in front to show an under-dress of gold color; small pointed cap of gold color and large white ruff.

MARIANA—Deep violet gown with train; band round the hair, which is either hanging loose or in two braids.

LADY MACBETH—Full Highland costume.

VIOLA—Long semi-fitting crimson gown with full length sleeves; puffings to show at elbow; gold cord and tassels brought twice around the waist and knotted at side.

STAGE SETTING AND PROPERTIES.

Room with antique chairs and tables; one table near center; mirrors and suffrage mottoes on walls; door at either side. Punch bowl, glasses, church warden or corncob pipes, tobacco jars, turpentine, grape juice, cider, sauce bottles and pepper pods, punch ladle, etc. Note for Grumio. Telephone attachment outside.

The Scotch songs used are familiar to everybody. "There's a Club House in the Town," sang [sic] by the Duke, is the old "There is a Tavern in the Town," which can be found in "College Songs," published by Oliver Ditson Co., which we will send postpaid on receipt of price, 50 cents.

STAGE DIRECTIONS.

R. means right of stage; *C.*, center; *L.*, left; *R. D.*, right door, etc. The actor is supposed to be facing the audience.

RE-TAMING OF THE SHREW

RE-TAMING OF THE SHREW

SCENE: Room in **PETRUCHIO'S** house; banners on the walls with mottoes, "Votes for Women," "Down with Rum," "Men are Tyrants All," "Matrimony is Slavery," "Our Battle Cry is Freedom." Doors R. and L. Antique chairs and tables; one table near C.

> *[*KATHERINE *and* MARIANA *enter R. and L., salute each other with kisses and sit down.]*

KATHERINE: The knell has sounded. Mere man is doomed.

MARIANA: And yet, Kate, I do not altogether blame the men. They are as God made them.

KATHERINE: Not so, Mariana. Shake off the influence of the moated grange. They are what our stupid submission made them—selfish, narrow-minded brutes, wine bibbers and brawlers, villains and hypocrites, sordid knaves and boasting bullies.

MARIANA: I can scarcely agree with you in that, sister. Some of them have good points, and a man means so much to most of us.

KATHERINE: *[sarcastically]*. I cry you mercy, Mariana. I had forgotten.

MARIANA: Forgotten what, darling?

KATHERINE: How thou fretted and pined and pleaded for Angelo, grabbed him with gratitude with all the horrid imperfections on his head.

MARIANA: *[warmly]*. And what of Petruchio, Kate, dear? He wooed thee like a madcap ruffian and swearing jack, and yet thou kissed his feet.

KATHERINE: Do not let us wrangle, Mariana. That was before I joined the suffragists. You ought to see him now.

> *[Enter* DESDEMONA, *R. They embrace and kiss and sit down.]*

DESDEMONA: You look flustered, Kate. Methought you were quarreling as I came in.

KATHERINE: Why, the idea! We quarrel?

MARIANA: How absurd!

DESDEMONA: Stranger things have happened in the woman's world. You certainly were speaking in pitched tones.

KATHERINE: Don't be sarcastic, dear. Pitched tones, indeed! One would think Othello was still on thy mind.

MARIANA: Yes, that thou wert still pillowed on his sooty bosom.

DESDEMONA: [protesting]. That is uncalled for, Mariana. "Pillowed" strikes me as unnecessarily harsh.

KATHERINE: [ironically]. I should imagine it did. You were smothered for a time, weren't you, dear?

> [DESDEMONA bounces angrily from her chair. Before she can make reply, LADY MACBETH enters L. and there is kissing all round.]

LADY MACBETH: I fancied ravens were croaking as I entered.

KATHERINE: Your imagination is too strong, dear. You should curtail it in time. First thing you know, you'll be walking in your sleep.

MARIANA: There was a frightful croak under your battlements once, I believe.

LADY MACBETH: Yes; I thank God I am a strong-minded woman.

DESDEMONA: With a passion for perfumery.

LADY MACBETH: I just love it, Desdemona.

DESDEMONA: You must, or you wouldn't try to wash your little hands in it.

LADY MACBETH: Well, of all the impudence!

DESDEMONA: No offense, your ladyship; none in the world. I was thinking of that damned spot that wouldn't wash out.

LADY MACBETH: It is very sweet of you, indeed, gentle Desdemona. But your optics and reflectives went astray when you eloped with that blackamoor.

KATHERINE: *[shocked]*. Lady Macbeth!

MARIANA: How rude and shocking!

LADY MACBETH: *[angrily]*. You spiteful wretches! It ill becomes any one of you to rake up a noble lady's past. But what can you expect of—

[This speech is interrupted by the entrance of **VIOLA***, R. More kissing.]*

VIOLA: Why this confusion, sisters? Your damask cheeks seem to be unduly incardinated.

KATHERINE: Your discernment is at fault this time, Viola. We were not confused. We were just having a pleasant preliminary chat.

VIOLA: And how is Petruchio, Katherine? I haven't seen the dear man since he sealed his title to you with a resounding kiss.

KATHERINE: Petruchio is as well as can be expected, dear. He is sitting, like Patience, rocking the cradle and smiling at grief.

MARIANA: That remark is not strictly original, Kate. I've heard something like it before.

LADY MACBETH: *[in warning tones]*. Pray stop there, Mariana.

KATHERINE: Yes, go no farther on that line. It is not meet that we, the sisterhood of sweet and sympathetic souls, should exchange personalities, however refreshing and delightful they may be. We are engaged in a noble cause. We should set the men an inspiring example in all things. Complete enfranchisement is within our reach. Let us rise to the occasion for the benefit and advancement of mankind.

VIOLA: That's the ticket. Enthuse us some more, Kate.

KATHERINE: We must prove ourselves faithful to the common cause. We must not waste ammunition on ourselves. We are going to look big, and stamp, and swear, and stare, and fret, just like the men used to do in the dismal days of the dreary past. We are going to show them that we are no longer their goods and chattels. We'll eat what we like, drink what we like, when we like and where we like. No longer shall they superintend the making of our beds, or fling the pillows, bolsters and coverlets around with angry snorts. They shall not deter us with threatening, unkind brows and scornful scowls. We shall show them that we are as free as the unchartered air; that the olive branch has vanished in the smoke of our righteous war; that henceforth, now and forever we shall retain the reins of state and domestic government in our firm and unrelaxing hands, and compel their unswerving obedience to all our imperious commands.

ALL: Amen!

[Enter GRUMIO, l. Curtseys to them all.]

GRUMIO: Master says will you please mitigate your voices. He's afraid you'll wake the baby.

KATHERINE: Go bid your master mind his own business. Let him rock the cradle diligently is the child is restless.

GRUMIO: Yes, Ma'am. *[Curtseys and exits, L.]*

VIOLA: You have him broken very nicely, Kate.

KATHERINE: Yes, his stomach is now completely vailed.

LADY MACBETH: How did you work the miracle?

KATHERINE: Oh, it was simple enough. When he blustered, I nagged him quiet. I hindered his sleep with sighs and moans, sauced him meat with upbraidings, spoiled his sports by brawling. As soon as his digestion was ruined, he begged for mercy on his marrow bones.

ALL: Wonderful!

LADY MACBETH: There's nothing like a good tongue lashing to bring them to time.

DESDEMONA: *[putting handkerchief to her eyes].* Oh, I wish I had known it sooner. What anguish I might have checked.

VIOLA: How grateful I am that the Duke is a Southern gentleman.

MARIANA: Neither climate nor color counts in these matters, dear. There are ferocious husbands in the North as well as the South.

KATHERINE: My experience is that they are all fanged like serpents.

LADY MACBETH: Yes, and their venomed clamors poison more deadly than a mad dog's tooth.

MARIANA: *[slyly].* You found daggers very useful, didn't you, dear?

LADY MACBETH: Daggers, strong words and drugged drinks were my favorite recipes.

KATHERINE: And is Macbeth still a prosperous gentleman?

LADY MACBETH: Not so as you would notice. It was all I could do to keep his courage at the sticking place. Banquo's ghost nearly scared the life out of him.

DESDEMONA: Well, Othello, rough as he was, always had his pluck about him.

LADY MACBETH: Yes, he showed it by deft manipulation of the feather pillow.

DESDEMONA: *[hotly].* You are perfectly horrid. Your braw Scotch laddie had to have a bracer for the murder of Duncan.

KATHERINE: Ladies, ladies! It ill beseems us to quarrel. Look at the mottoes on the walls.

[They turn and read and wave handkerchiefs.]

DESDEMONA: We never thought of quarreling, Kate. We were just comparing notes.

MARIANA: Comparisons are odorous [sic], dear. The best of men are moulded out of faults, and I know one who became much the better for being a little bad.

LADY MACBETH: She means that puritanical hypocrite, Angelo.

MARIANA: *[warmly]*. Truth is sometimes spoken in the spite. With all his faults, my husband never traded with witches on a blasted heath at midnight, mid thunder, lightning and rain.

KATHERINE: Come, come, ladies! Do not let us brawl about our husbands. They are all bad enough, the Lord knows, and our dearest purpose now is to redeem and reform them. I move we lay them on the table.

ALL: Carried unanimously!

[Enter GRUMIO, L., and presents note to KATHERINE.]

KATHERINE: Listen to this, girls. *[Reads note]*: "Baby is sleeping finely, Katherine. While you are at the club this evening, will you please allow me to have a friend or two in, so that I may not be lonesome during your absence. Your humble spouse, Petruchio."

MARIANA: What a darling of a man!

LADY MACBETH: Vouchsafe him permission, Kate. Solitude sometimes gets on the nerves. I know what I suffered when sitting up of Macbeth.

KATHERINE: Tell thy master, Grumio, that his request is granted, but that his company must be dismissed by ten o'clock. Should I still be out at that time, see him safely tucked in bed.

GRUMIO: Who? The baby?

KATHERINE: No, stupid; thy master.

GRUMIO: Yes, ma'am. *[Exit L.]*

KATHERINE: Let us now repair to the club. A little bridge or tango will do us all good.

[The ladies primp up at mirrors and then go our R., chattering.]

[Enter GRUMIO, *L., and two or three servants.]*

GRUMIO: Now that the cats are away, the mice may play. Get the place ready for a rip-roaring time. The old boys are somewhat weary of this woman-bossed world. They'd fain have a taste of the old life.

> *[Servants arrange chairs at table, bringing in punch bowl, pipes, tobaacco jars, glasses, etc., and retire L.* PETRUCHIO *enters L. with apron on and nursing bottle strung round his neck. Takes off aprong, throws it aside with a frown, puts nursing bottle on table and sniffs at bowl.]*

PETRUCHIO: Is this the best of our cheer?

GRUMIO: 'Tis furnished as Mistress Katherine commanded, sir—good, honest barley water, that ne'er left man i' the mire.

PETRUCHIO: You flap-headed knave, we cannot be merry on barley-water. Throw it out and fill the bowl with sack.

GRUMIO: Forsooth, I dare not for my life.

PETRUCHIO: Dare not? Who's boss here?

GRUMIO: My mistress, sir.

PETRUCHIO: Jumping Jeosophat [sic], have I no rights left? Hast lost thy wit entirely? We must have wholesome liquor.

GRUMIO: Mistress Katherine says barley-water or nothing. 'Tis a palatable, nourishing beverage, sir. But what say you to small ale?

PETRUCHIO: Small ale! Ye gods, am I Christopher Sly the tinker? And yet 'tis better than this cold, cheerless stuff.

GRUMIO: A dish of ale is fit for a king, sir.

PETRUCHIO: And so it may be when occasion serves. Well, bring it in, good Grumio.

GRUMIO: *[mockingly].* Ah! It's good Grumio now! Erstwhile I was knave and rascal and caressed with they bootjack. And now you speak soft and beg for small ale.

PETRUCHIO: *[sternly]*. Do not provoke a down-trodden man, sirrah. The power of assertion may rise again and crush thee with its might. Do as I bid thee, or, by Jupiter, I'll break they wooden noddle.

GRUMIO: Mitigate your voice, sir. The club is only on the next block.

PETRUCHIO: *[trembling]*. Dost think she could hear me, Grumio? I had forgotten the club house is so near. But the small ale, man; the small ale, an thou be a Christian.

GRUMIO: I fear it is too choleric, sir. What say you to a bottle of Worcestershire sauce?

PETRUCHIO: Excellent, i' faith; there's some grip to sauce.

GRUMIO: Maybe it is too hot. There is a bottle of bluing in the laundry, sir.

PETRUCHIO: Bluing? Heavens! I am blue enough as it is; but anything to give tone to our spirits.

GRUMIO: Well, I don't know. Perhaps you had better have the bottle without the bluing.

PETRUCHIO: Thou false, deluding knave. [Rushing toward him.] Get thee gone ere I break they numbskull.

[GRUMIO *rushes out in alarm, L.]*

[Enter **MACBETH**, *singing:*]

MACBETH: Gie me the greatest joy the tongue o' man can name,

A bonnie, bonnie lassie when the kye come hame.

PETRUCHIO: Hail, thane of Cawdor! King that is to be!

MACBETH: Hoot mon! The thane of Cawdor is no deid yet, and to be king stands not iwthin the prospect of belief. Ye've eaten of the insane root, Pete, my lad. Your heid is out o' kilter.

PETRUCHIO: Well, present fears are less than horrible imaginings, Mac. You're safe enough now; the witches have fled.

MACBETH: Then shall we hae anither gaudy nicht, ech, mon?

PETRUCHIO: We shall, indeed, if barley-water can assure it.

MACBETH: What? Hast barley bree? Guid Scotch drink is nectar for any sensible stomach. *[Warbles.]* "And aye we'll taste the barley bree."

    [Enter ANGELO, *L.]*

PETRUCHIO: Mortality and mercy live in thy tongue and heart, dear old chap.

MACBETH: Thy company transports me beyond this ignorant present, and I feel now the future in the instant.

ANGELO: Thanks, noble comrades. I have with a leavened and prepared choice proceeded to you.

    [Enter the DUKE, *L.]*

PETRUCHIO: Welcome, your grace. Methinks thou purgest the air of pestilence.

MACBETH: Come, let me clutch thee. *[Takes the* DUKE'S *hand.]* Ah! Thou art sensible to feeling as to sight, a blessing to sair een!

ANGELO: Now may we play such tricks before high heaven as will make the suffragists weep.

THE DUKE: Oh, spirit of brotherly love! When suffragists' shafts have killed the flock of all affections else, thy sweet perfections will make a paradise below.

    [Enter OTHELLO, *L.]*

PETRUCHIO: Oh, my fair warrior! It gives me wonder great as my content to hae thou join our festivities.

ANGELO: My soul's joy! If after every tempest come such guests, may the winds blow till they have wakened death. My hungry heart greets thee without cloyment or revolt.

THE DUKE: If it were now to die, noble Othello, 'twere now to be most happy; for I fear my soul hath her content so absolute that not another comfort like to this succeeds in unknown fate.

MACBETH: Blow wind, come wrack! Now we'll keep the harness on our back.

OTHELLO: Most potent, grave and reverend seigniors, my very bovle and approved companions, I greet ye all with constant breath. But what sense I here? *[Looking at bowl.]* That bowl is inviting.

PETRUCHIO: Come, sit ye down. Ye shall not budge till that the conquering wine steeps your souls in sofe and delicate lethe.

> *[All take places at table.* **PETRUCHIO** *ladles out the drink. They clink glasses and toss off the contents. Then they sputter nad make wry faces and gaze at* **PETRUCHIO** *reproachfully.]*

MACBETH: Barley without the bree!

THE DUKE: Adam's toddy, as I'm a Dago!

OTHELLO: A disgusting fraud on honest thirst.

ANGELO: An insult to sacred friendship.

PETRUCHIO: I pray ye, do not mock me, fellow sufferers; 'tis all I'm permitted to offer.

MACBETH: The guards of Duncan's chamber were primed with stiffer stuff.

ANGELO: It makes a vice of marriment.

THE DUKE: A mockery of kitchen slops.

OTHELLO: Too soulless for the trade of war.

MACBETH: For the love of auld Scotia, send for a stoop of usquebagh.

PETRUCHIO: Bear with me yet awhile; I'll see what can be done. Grumio!

> *[Enter* **GRUMIO***, L., grinning.]*

GRUMIO: Here, sir.

PETRUCHIO: My guests like not this vile decoction, sirrah. Go thou and thy fellows and scour the ward for sturdy liquor. Get us something with fire and comfort in it.

GRUMIO: Mistress said I was not to leave the house while the carousal was on.

PETRUCHIO: Carousal! Was ever word so abused? Zounds, rascal, I'll swinge thee soundly an thou do not instantly obey me.

GRUMIO: 'Tis as much as my life is worth, and I have not prayed tonight.

[PETRUCHIO makes threatening gesture.]

But I'll venture all for this gallant company.

PETRUCHIO: And see here, sirrah. Take this bauble *[handing him nursing bottle]* and have it filled with soothing syrup; thou knowest the brand.

GRUMIO: 'Twill bring disaster, master. She can scent the fumes in a corncob. *[Exit L.]*

ALL: Poor Petruchio!

PETRUCHIO: And now, friends, we'll drink some tobacco while the knaves are about it.

[They charge and light pipes, but lay them down with scorn after a few puffs.]

MACBETH: Shades of auld Reekie; 'tis cabbage leaf!

THE DUKE: Holy smoke, how it bites!

ANGELO: Mouldy hay were sweeter, methinks.

OTHELLO: Ratsbane, if I'm any judge.

PETRUCHIO: Wrong, all of you. 'Tis tea leaves sprinkled with nutmeg!

ALL: Poor Petruchio!

MACBETH: Bear up, brave hearts. I've the real stingo in my pouch. *[Reaches into his philibeg and brings out package.]* Fill full and smoke to the general health of the whole table.

> *[They charge pipes with* **MACBETH'S** *tobacco, light up and puff away in content.]*

> *[Enter* **GRUMIO** *and other servants with packages.]*

GRUMIO: *[in alarm].* As I live, they are smoking tobacco! Master, master! What will Mistress Kate say? It will cling to the hangings for a week.

OTHELLO: May I answer, Petruchio?

PETRUCHIO: Go as far as you like, Otto. I'm too furious to speak!

OTHELLO: Mistress Katherine be hanged!

ALL: So say all of us!

GRUMIO: But Desdemona is with her, General; and Mariana and Viola and Lady Macbeth.

ALL: *[in dismay].* Oh!

PETRUCHIO: Courage, lads. New blood is springing in my veins. They won't be home till morning.

ALL: *[sing].* "Till daylight does appear!" Hurrah!

PETRUCHIO: How fared thou with the tradesmen, Grumio?

GRUMIO: Very scurvily, sir. The groceryman said Mistress Katherine had warned him against supplying us with liquor except by her written order, and he is afraid of punishment under the dram shop act should he disobey. The apothecary—a lean and hungry cadaver, your honor—insisted upon a doctor's description; the furniture man had nothing on hand but turpentine, and all we could get from the vegetable man was root beer. We have here, therefore, a pint of turpentine, a bottle of ginger ale, a quart of sweet cider, and bottle of denatured alcohol, some pepper pods, and a quart of grape juice; the same kind that Mr. Bryan uses, sir.

ALL: Oh, balm of Gilead!

PETRUCHIO: Well, anything is better than sheer barley-water. Drop them all into the bowl.

[Servants pour in contents of bottles and **GRUMIO** *stirs briskly.]*

GRUMIO: I got this *[handing PETRUCHIO nursing bottle filled with dark liquid]* after much vehement protest. The clerk said it was not altogether to be commended for babies, but I calmed his fears with the solemn assurance that it was for a big one.

ALL: Ha, ha!

[**PETRUCHIO** *smell at nursing bottle. A smile overspreads his face and he puts it hastily into his pocket.]*

PETRUCHIO: I am afraid of that stuff. It's rank poison.

GRUMIO: That's what mistress says, sir.

PETRUCHIO: Silence, sirrah!

[Telephone bell rings. **GRUMIO** *goes out and returns as* **PETRUCHIO** *is ladling out the new mixture.]*

GRUMIO: Mistress says to be sure and give baby his bottle if he wakes up.

PETRUCHIO: I'll be hanged if I will!

ALL: There's manly courage for you!

GRUMIO: Shall I tell her what you say, sir?

PETRUCHIO: Not on your life, sirrah. Tell her I will be very careful that tootsey-wootsey sleeps well and that I hope she is wnjoying herself.

ALL: Ha, ha!

[Exit **GRUMIO***, L.]*

MACBETH: *[after drinking].* It's no so bad.

OTHELLO: Not as searching as canary; but 'twill serve.

ANGELO: I've tasted worse, but not much.

THE DUKE: Scarcely up to the Illyrian standard, but nevertheless strong and biting.

PETRUCHIO: I think it is celestial liquor. Fill full again.

[Replenishes cups. Liquor begins to take effect as they continue drinking.]

ANGLEO: Gives us a song, Mac.

MACBETH: *[sings].*

[Tune: "Annie Laurie."]

Maxwelton's braes are bonnie,
As bonnie as can be;
And 'twas there where Annie Laurie
Gie me the barley bree;
Gie me the barley bree,
As grand as it could be,
And for bonnie Annie Laurie,
I drank that barley bree!

[All applaud as glasses are refilled.]

OTHELLO: 'Fore heaven, a most excellent song!

PETRUCHIO: It's your turn now, Duke.

THE DUKE: *[sings].*

[Tune: "There is a Tavern in the Town."]

There's a club-house in the town, in the town,
And there our dear wives sit them down, sit them down,
And drink their wine 'mid laughter free,
And never, never think of we!

[Chorus.]

Fare thee well, for I must leave thee;
Do not let the parting grieve thee,
And remember that the best of friends much part, must part;
Adieu, adieu, kind friends; adieu, adieu, adieu!
I can no longer stay with you, stay with you;

I'll hang my harp on a weeping willow tree,
And may the world go well with thee!

OTHELLO: Why, that is a more excellent song than the other.

MACBETH: Easy there, Otto. Remember Bobby Burns.

ANGELO: What for?

MACBETH: I dinna comprehend your query, man.

ANGELO: You said Bobby Burns. Why?

MACBETH: [puzzled]. Eh?

PETRUCHIO: Don't you see, Mac? It's a way he has of joking.

OTHELLO: It's dangerous to joke with a scotchman.

THE DUKE: Doubly so, if you haven't a corkscrew.

> [All laugh but MACBETH.]

MACBETH: [angry]. Ye puir fackless bodies; an ye were on the heath, I'd clout your lugs wi' my claymore.

PETRUCHIO: Suspend, gentlemen, suspend! Don't let us act like women at a love feast. Let harmony and kindness prevail. We'll have another wet.

> [Cups are charged again and they drink after touching glasses. GRUMIO enters L. and whispers to PETRUCHIO.]

OTHELLO: Methinks our gallant host turns pale.

MACBETH: That's more than ye can do, Otto.

OTHELLO: [hotly]. Death and damnation, sir!

MACBETH: [snapping his fingers]. Tilly vally, Otto; sneck up; you're no in Venice the noo.

PETRUCHIO: Peace, gentlemen, peace! Grumio says they are breaking up at the club. They'll make a bee-line here; but there's time for a doch and doris, as Mac calls it.

[Glasses are filled hurriedly.]

MACBETH: We'll part in the guid auld way. Let's hae the Scotch doxology. Hand in hand and round the table go. Then a recht guid wullie-wacht and awa hame!

[All take hands and sing loudly, "Should Auld Acquaintance be Forgot."]

[Enter **KATHERINE, LADY MACBETH, VIOLA, MARIANA** *and* **DESDEMONA***, R. The men slink to other side of room.]*

KATHERINE: *[indignant].* Phew! What an atmosphere! Is it thus *[speaking to* **PETRUCHIO***]* you abuse your privileges, sir? Do you dare to make a tavern of my house? Have you people no wit, manners, or modesty, but to squeak out vile songs without remorse of voice?

MACBETH: It was no a vile song, begging your ladyship's pardon. It's a masterpiece of mellifluous melody, the pride of the Scottish race, and the pledge of good fellowship a' the wairld o'er.

LADY MACBETH: *[astonished].* Macbeth, how dare you?

MACBETH: *[boldly].* Dare! I'd dare the Deil himself on that theme.

LADY MACBETH: Wait till I get you home.

MACBETH: *[more boldly].* Pshaw! Shake not your linty locks at me. There's no terror in those eyes with which you glare. Thou canst say that I did it, and that I'm glad of it!

KATHERINE, VIOLA, MARIANA and DESDEMONA: Mercy, the man's mad!

LADY MACBETH: No, not mad, sisters; just a drappie in his een. I know the complaint of old. He'll come to himself tomorrow, and be mild enough, I warrant you.

ANGELO: Dollars to doughnuts he won't.

MARIANA: *[in amazement].* Why, Angelo, what have you been drinking?

ANGELO: Nothing but barley-water, pet; it's all we can get in this shanty.

KATHERINE: Cast no aspersions upon my house, sir. It was by my expres command that barley-water was served.

THE DUKE: *[scornfully].* And it served us right for coming.

VIOLA: *[in protesting tone].* Orsino, don't be rude. I've never seen you like this before.

THE DUKE: *[boldly].* You will again, I hope. Let's have that strain once more boys. It came o'er my ears like the sweet sound tha breathes upon a bank of violets, stealing and giving odor—

VIOLA: *[amazed].* Why, I do believe his grace is intoxicated.

OTHELLO: *[with a sneer].* What! On barley-water?

DESDEMONA: *[gently].* Don't you chip in, Othello. They draw the color line in these parts.

OTHELLO: *[angry].* Toads and monkeys! Would I had used a clothes line instead of a pillow.

DESDEMONA: *[irritated].* Comfort forswear me! I hate you when you gnaw your nether lip like that.

KATHERINE: Stand you there like a sheep, Petruchio, in the face of this outrageous contention. I took you for a man, once.

PETRUCHIO: Well, 'twas you that made me a mutton.

KATHERINE: I?

PETRUCHIO: *[angry].* Ay, thou! Why did I not heed the warning of they kinsfold? They told me thou weeert a curst shrew. Madman that I was, I rushed wildly to my fate.

KATHERINE: *[puts hand to bosom].* Oh, my bleeding heart! Give me the nursing bottle and I will go to my babe.

[PETRUCIO hands it to her. KATHERINE smells it and screams:]

You murderous wretch! This is whiskey. Oh, my baby, my baby! Grumio, take me to my poor child.

GRUMIO: Calm yourself, my lady; that is soothing syrup. I bought it myslef, but the child has not yet tasted it.

KATHERINE: Bless thee for tha assurance. But how came they all drunk?

THE MEN: It's a lie!

PETRUCHIO: We are not drunk; we are simply indignant.

KATHERINE: Indignant?

THE MEN: Ay, indignant.

PETRUCHIO: We rebelled at they imposed cheer, as we now rebel against all forms of feminine tyranny. Grown men cannot thrive on barley-water, whether the state be dry or not.

 [KATHERINE *goes to the bowl, dips in ladle and tastes the liquid.*]

KATHERINE: [*startled*]. What kind of hell broth is this?

PETRUCHIO: A little of everything drinkable—ginger ale, grape juice, turpentine, furniture polish and laundry bluing, garnished with red pepper pods.

LADY MACBETH: No wonder the men are mad.

PETRUCHIO: [*stoutly*]. Right-o! We are mad! We have come to the parting of the ways. You can have your suffrage, your votes, your clubs, your political freedom. But we have thrown away the bibs and tuckers. We wear the aprons and flourish the dusters no longer. Henceforth we are free.

THE MEN: Hurrah!

KATHERINE: This is rank rebellion, sisters, and must be suppressed with prompt and rigorous measures. Let us go into executive session.

[Male and female characters form two groups at either side of the room. GRUMIO takes a seat in front of punch bowl. Turns first to one group and then the other; drinks at each demonstration and wags his head. Great excitement in the female group. The men gesticulate and cast furtive glances at their wives. KATHERINE steps forward.]

KATHERINE: I will be frank with you, gentlemen, and say that the attitude you have assumed tonight both shocked and surprised us. We may have been a little stern with you of late, butr modern civilization calls for the assertion of our rights. If persistence in our just demands leads to insurrection on your part, we acknowledge that the peace and joy of the world will not be advanced. My sisters think a compromise is in order. I pause for your response.

[The men urge PETRUCHIO forward to answer.]

PETRUCHIO: What have you to propose?

KATHERINE: Let us keep the ballot and maintain our interest in public affairs. 'Tis for your own good that we seek this power.

[The men consult again.]

PETRUCHIO: The proposition is too indefinite. Do you demand that we give up all our rights and privilieges?

[The women confer.]

KATHERINE: We propose tha whatever rights you are justly entitled to you may enjoy without let or hindrance.

[The men consult.]

PETRUCHIO: Will you bar prohibition, abolish nurse girl duties, sanction cards and billiards, bowls and baseball, and place no restrictions on our club duties?

[The women again consult.]

KATHERINE: We cannot agree to your program.

PETRUCHIO: Then we shall appeal to the divorce court for a dissolution of matrimonial ties and restoration of our ancient rights nad privileges.

[*Consternation among the women.*]

MARIANA: Isn't that awful, Katie? I had a hard time getting Angelo.

KATHERINE: To agree to that would be a base surrender of honor s already won.

DESDEMONA: Yes, but beggarly divorcement! I think we must give in. I don't think I could live without my Othello.

VIOLA: I don't want to play Patience on the monument again. It's a cold and thankless part.

MARIANA: And we'd all be grass widows!

VIOLA, DESDEMONA and LADY MACBETH: Heaven preserve us!

KATHERINE: Let me temporize with them. We may yet—

[*As **KATHERINE** steps forward to address the men, the other women drag her back.*]

PETRUCHIO: We await your answer, fair dames.

THE WOMEN: We agree!

PETRUCHIO: With full and free conscience? Without mental reservation?

THE WOMEN: [*sobbing*]. Yes.

THE MEN: Hurrah!

THE DUKE: 'Tis love that makes the world go round.

KATHERINE: And you will treat us with the tender consideration of yore?

THE MEN: We swear!

KATHERINE: But we don't want you to swear.

PETRUCHIO: We must. The deal will be off if we can't.

THE WOMEN: Then swear.

THE MEN: Hurrah, boys, hurrah!

KATHERINE: You have won, gentlemen. See that you make good use of the conquest. Remember the whirligig of time continues to spin and that in the final trial justice plays no favorties. And now good night all.

> *[The men embrace their wives and, with the exception of* **KATHERINE** *and* **PETRUCHIO**, *go off the stage in couples.* **GRUMIO** *attends each couple in stately fashion, retiring himself at last with a wave of his hand toward his master.* **PETRUCHIO** *and* **KATHERINE** *step to the front. She hands him the nursing bottle.]*

Here, my big baby, is your soothing syrup.

PETRUCHIO: And this is yours, sweetheart and wife! *[Kisses her.]*

CURTAIN.

www.ingramcontent.com/pod-product-compliance
Lightning Source LLC
Chambersburg PA
CBHW022306060426
42446CB00007BA/730